W9-AOY-727

2614

THE CASE AGAINST DOGMA

THE CASE AGAINST DOGMA

GERALD O'COLLINS, S.J.

ST. JOSEPH'S UNIVERSITY STX
BTQ 29 .O25
The case against dogma /
3 9353 00156 0075

PAULIST PRESS
New York / Paramus / Toronto

157556

Published by Paulist Press
Editorial Office: 1865 Broadway, N.Y., N.Y. 10023
Business Office: 400 Sette Drive, Paramus, N.J. 07652

All rights reserved No part of this book may be
reproduced or transmitted in any form or by any
means, electronic or mechanical, including photo-
copying, recording or by any information storage
and retrieval system, without permission in writing
from the Publisher.

ISBN 0–8091–1853–x

Library of Congress Catalog Card Number:
74–15495

Copyright © Gerald O'Collins, 1975

Printed and bound in Great Britain

Nihil Obstat: Rev. Mgr. Matthew P. Stapleton
Imprimatur: ✠ Humberto Cardinal Medeiros
Archbishop of Boston
September 19, 1974

To Richard and Bridget
dear friends

We know that our minds have been formed by the conventions of our present language and social institutions, and that we can only achieve a certain degree of detachment from them, even by the utmost efforts of reflection and comparison.

Stuart Hampshire, *Thought and Action*

Contents

Introduction, xi

Chapter I   Terminology, 1
Chapter II   The Case Against Dogma, 9
Chapter III   Functions of Dogma, 23
Chapter IV   Limiting and Defending Dogma, 39
Chapter V   Boundaries and Meaning, 68
Chapter VI   The End of 'Dogma'?, 86

Notes, 101
Very Select Bibliography, 107
Index of Names, 109

Introduction

HAVE CHRISTIAN DOGMAS a future? Or should we abandon any attempt to retain or even make sense of those normative statements of belief which past Christians have left to us? In a given tradition the dogmatic inheritance may be minimal, and not include much more than the account of Christ as one (divine) person in two natures. Through those terms the Council of Chalcedon (A.D 451) sought to 'define' the relationship of his humanity and divinity. Or, as is the case with Roman Catholics, we may have inherited a long history of dogmas stretching down through such councils as Trent (1545–68) and Vatican I (1869–70) to Pope Pius XII's definition of the bodily assumption of the Virgin Mary into heaven (1950. What points of value and truth for Christian living emerge from all those solemn declarations of belief, which bishops, popes and other Church leaders have bequeathed to Christians in the late twentieth century?

Several options are open to us. Many past dogmas may strike us as misguided and erroneous attempts to pin down God's revelation in Christ. They have diminished rather than enhanced the stature of the Gospel message, falsified rather than clarified its appeal. Or these doctrines may come across as noble but irrelevant monuments from the past. To echo Thomas Mann, they are like deserted houses, still impressive but uninhabited. Or again we may find that it is possible to construe past dogmas in a way that allows them to play some role today as 'guides and incentives to Christian living'.[1]

My search for a well-considered position on dogmas could look like a trip towards a pedantic dead end, a waste of energy in the face of more pressing responsibilities. However, this search remains one of the major tasks in our coming to terms with Christian history and its meaning. Whether we end up viewing those dogmas as destructive, divisive, irrelevant or open to creative reinterpretation, nothing is to be gained by quietly ignoring them and deciding that for us Christian life begins in 1974. Such attempts to make an absolute break with the past and deny any present significance to our history, dogmatic or otherwise, put us in an impossible position. We will only once again illustrate the axiom attributed to George Santayana to the effect that 'those who refuse to learn from history are compelled to repeat it'.

The post-World War II period has witnessed much theological debate about the development of dogma and, more generally, the development of doctrine. Owen Chadwick, Henri de Lubac, Jaroslav Pelikan, Karl Rahner and others have contributed notably to this debate.[2] A revived concern with John Henry Newman's *Essay on the Development of Christian Doctrine* accompanied and encouraged this debate. Hans Küng's *Infallible? An Enquiry*[3] occasioned a flood of writing on the Church's authority to issue infallibly true pronouncements.[4] The debates about development and infallibility have presupposed attitudes towards the nature and function of dogmas. But the focus of interest has often not been dogma as such. The valuable studies on that topic have frequently concentrated on dogma as an ecumenical problem (Avery Dulles and Edmund Schlink). Or they have taken up the specific charge that dogmas represent an unfortunate, or at best temporary, 'Hellenization' of the Christian message.[5] There has been a lack of attention to the way dogmas work, as well as a readiness to use conventional terms like 'the meaning of dogmas' and 'dogmatic history' (*Dogmengeschichte*) which gloss over severe problems. Whose meaning are we to accept when examining any given dogma? Doubtless, those who agreed on a given formulation at any Church Council would, if questioned, have usually offered us different paraphrases of what was meant. Is 'dogma' a dubious classification which wrongly fixes boundaries and too easily supposes an historical stream, uniform in all its points? 'Dogma' is a recent category. We apply it to Chalcedon and Trent by a retrospective hypothesis, which may falsely imply a simple, great series in which every dogma would assume its place.

How can we usefully initiate our discussion? After clarifying various terminological details, it seems advisable to rehearse some of the major objections to a dogmatic Christianity. This is not undertaken as an empty gesture, but out of respect for the challenges from Adolf Harnack, Bertrand Russell and others. Only by hearing the case against dogma can we hope to refrain from taking too much for granted and elaborate anything like a sensitive account of how dogmas might usefully work in practice. There is an acute need for a much more discriminating approach than those normally offered, if dogmas are not only to survive but also to enhance Christian life. We may, of course, decide to eliminate the category of dogma and describe authoritative Christian teaching in more serviceable terms.

In this book I will use as my examples Roman Catholic dogmas. But much of what is to be argued will apply easily to the Augsburg Confession, the Formula of Concord, the Thirty-Nine Articles, the Westminster Confession and other official statements of faith considered normative by Protestant and Anglican churches.

I would like to express my sincere thanks to John Coventry, Nicholas Lash, Hugh Mellor, Josef Nolte, Patrick Sherry and Professor Maurice Wiles for the help of some valuable discussion. I am grateful to the Master and Fellows of my college. They welcomed me back with warm kindness, and provided the material support for a happy sabbatical year which produced this book. Finally, my thanks are due to Mrs Verna Cole for her care and skill in typing this manuscript.

With permission a very small amount of material has been taken from my *Foundations of Theology* (Loyola University Press, 1971) and *The Easter Jesus* (Darton, Longman and Todd, 1973).

Pembroke College,   February 12, 1974
Cambridge.

1

Terminology

How CAN WE start to think and talk theologically about dogmas? To prevent this book from becoming confused and confusing from the outset, let us begin with some answerable, if less exhilarating, questions of terminology. How old is the notion of 'dogma' in Christian vocabulary? In what sense(s) do theologians and others understand and use this term?

It may surprise a few readers that dogma gained secure tenure in Christian, or at least Catholic, theological vocabulary only in the last hundred years. The word turns up occasionally in the New Testament. A dogma or decree 'went out from Caesar Augustus that all the world should be enrolled' (Lk 2:1). Paul and Timothy on their journey through the Christian communities of Asia Minor delivered the dogmas or decisions on moral matters which the apostles and elders had reached in Jerusalem: the gentile Christians were asked to 'abstain from what had been sacrificed to idols and from blood and from what was strangled and from unchastity' (Acts 15:29; 16:4). In New Testament usage dogma denotes instructions or decisions on practical issues. Church fathers like Augustine, Ambrose, Leo the Great and Gregory the Great gave the word a wide range of meaning and applied it even to false doctrines. On the one hand, Christ's command 'Love your enemies' was called a dogma. On the other hand, the third Council of Constantinople solemnly 'execrated' the 'impious dogmas' of the monothelites and Pope Honorius I who denied a human will in Christ (DS 551). The medieval theologians rarely spoke of dogma. Their closest term was *articulus fidei* (article of faith). The Council of Trent described its most authoritative conclusions as 'canons'. Tridentine dogmas were not necessarily revealed truths, but could be features of ecclesiastical discipline, fixed customs of the universal Church or simply established facts. Even as late as 1854 Pius IX used dogma in his allocution *Singulari quadam* synonymously with religious and philosophical truth. The day before this allocution he had solemnly defined the immaculate conception of the Virgin Mary, but he called this belief a 'revealed doctrine'.

Like the notions of *fides* and *haeresis* 'dogma' has undergone a process both of refinement and restriction of meaning. In the jargon of twentieth-century Catholic theology dogma has come to mean: (1) a divinely revealed truth, (2) proclaimed as such by the infallible teaching authority of the Church and (3) hence binding now and forever on all the faithful.[1] Let me develop these three elements in this description.

Only revealed truth which belongs to the 'deposit of faith' laid down finally by Christ and his apostles can become dogma. Two conclusions follow. First, the New Testament contains no dogmas in the proper sense of the term. The age of the apostles formed the constitutive phase of the Church and the time when foundational revelation closed. Dogmas belong to the interpretative phase of dependent revelation—to the continuing history of a Church which has fully come into existence and now looks back to its founding fathers, the apostles, and to the climax of revelation in Christ's life, death and resurrection. Second, what does not belong to that foundational revelation in Christ is ruled out as a candidate for dogmatic definition. Teaching on birth control, for instance, is excluded, because as such it does not involve revealed truth.

As regards (2), leaders in the Church, exercising their teaching office (*magisterium*), must authoritatively propose something as revealed truth, if it is to attain the status of dogma. They may do this formally by defining the truth. In an act of the 'extraordinary' *magisterium* a Council or Pope can solemnly proclaim that Christ 'instituted' seven Sacraments (the Council of Trent), or that the Virgin Mary through the anticipated merits of her Son was preserved free even from original sin (Pius IX). Dogmas may also be expressed in the ordinary day to day teaching of bishops and popes. It has never been formally defined that redemption comes through Christ. This truth is classified as belonging materially to Catholic faith (*de fide catholica*), but never explicitly formulated as a dogma (*de fide definita*). A table appended to this chapter illustrates more fully the terminology that has been commonly used here by Catholic theologians.

Authors commonly invoke two grounds to explain why dogmas are deemed irrevocably binding (3). The claim of God's truth revealed in Christ confronts us. The teaching officers in the Church enjoy divine authority in proclaiming dogmas. Sometimes it is added that the binding quality of dogma arises from the fact that it expresses 'the mind of the community'. John Macquarrie's description confines itself to this point: 'A dogma would seem to have at least three distinguishing marks: it has its basis in . . . revelation; it is proposed by the Church, as expressing the mind of the community on a particular issue; and it has a conceptual and propositional form, being often expressed in a philosophical terminology'.[2] In pratically every case 'the community' would have to be taken in a sense narrower than the total community of Christian believers. The Council of Trent obviously did not express the mind of all sixteenth-century Christians. In its statements about Christ the Council of Chalcedon failed to satisfy all sections of the Church. A large group (Monophysites) refused to accept the Chalcedonian confession. Neither Council could be said to have given voice to *the* mind of the community on the specific issues they dealt with. Macquarrie's explanation stops us from applying the term 'dogma' to practically any conciliar definition of importance, unless we are ready to restrict drastically the number of Christian minds which make up that elusive religious authority, the mind of the community. In their discussions of terminology most Catholic theologians have preferred to account for the normative quality of dogma by appealing to Church authority or divine truth rather than to some alleged consensus. Even J. H. Walgrave qualifies his phrase about 'the consensus of the Church' by introducing a 'generally' and adding an alternative explanation : 'Dogmas are such propositions about revealed truth as are *generally* accepted by the consensus of the Church *or* consecrated by a definition of its highest authority in matters of doctrine.'[3]

If we look at non-Catholic writers, we find that Pelikan prefers to ascribe the element of obligation in dogma to the authority of Church leaders. He describes dogmas as 'the normative statements of Christian belief adopted by various ecclesiastical authorities and enforced as the official teaching of the church'.[4] F. Loofs offers a similar account and notes that this control falls more heavily on theological teachers than on Christians at large. Dogmas are propositions of faith 'which an ecclesiastical community requires its members, or at least its teachers, to acknowledge'.[5] Harnack gives more prominence to the authority of God's truth and judgement. He writes : 'The dogmas of the church are the doctrines of the Christian faith logically formulated and expressed for scientific and apologetic purposes . . . They are regarded in the Christian churches as the truths . . . composing the *depositum fidei*, the acknowledgement of these truths being the precondition of the blessedness held in prospect by religion.'[6] Like Pelikan, Loofs and Harnack, most Catholic writers derive the binding nature of dogma either from (legitimate) authority in the Church or directly from God himself.

To clarify the way terminology has been and still is used we can complete this brief opening chapter by (a) comparing dogma with doctrine, and (b) noting the common, non-technical and pejorative sense of dogma. Everything that Christians believe, confess and teach can be labelled 'doctrine'. Every dogma is a doctrine, but obviously not every doctrine attains dogmatic status. G. K. Chesterton wrote a brief poem in a book of pictures which a young friend had received. The last stanza ran:

> Stand up and keep your childishness:
>> Read all the pedants' screeds and strictures;
> But don't believe in anything
>> That can't be told in coloured pictures.

It may be out of the question to introduce a coloured picture here, but a sketch could help.

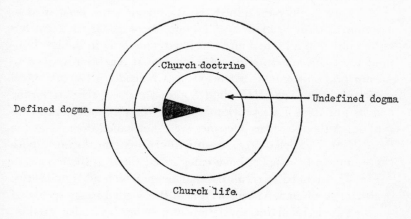

Church teaching forms only part of the full range of Christian life and activity. Within the circle of doctrine lies the circle of dogmas, both defined and undefined. Is there a difference of kind or only of degree between (1) 'mere' doctrines and (2) dogmas? Do we make a quantum jump when we pass from the second circle into the innermost circle? The way theologians interpret this relationship depends ultimately on their view of revelation itself. They all agree that what is not revealed cannot become a dogma.

However, some have understood the revelation given through Christ to be a divine manifestation of truths which would otherwise have remained inaccessible to human reason. Such a propositional view of revelation entails maintaining a strict difference of kind between dogmas and 'mere' doctrines. Those who interpret revelation as God's self-revealing encounter decline to draw hard and fast lines between Church doctrine and dogma. The possible ways in which God may speak to men and women through Christ cannot be pinned down in advance. We cannot confine divine revelation to an area of actual or potential dogmatic definitions, as if 'mere' Church doctrine formed no more than an outer, protective belt, which might be necessary for practical reasons but cannot mediate revelation.[7]

We have rapidly examined the way dogma has been used as a technical term in modern (Catholic) theology. If the term has settled down in a refined and restricted sense only in the last hundred years, by anachronistic classification it has been applied to solemn pronouncements as various as Chalcedon's Christological confession, Boniface VIII's bull *Unam Sanctam*, the Tridentine canons and Pius IX's proclamation of Mary's immaculate conception. Although these doctrines were not called dogmas at the time of their appearance, twentieth-century theologians, both Protestant and Catholic, have categorized them as such.

Finally, we need to recall popular usage which adds pejorative overtones to dogma. Where technical theological usage speaks of dogma's basis in divine revelation and its authoritative quality, popular usage suggests tenets which are not only irrational and arbitrary but also an affront to human freedom. Like the dogmas of Marxism the dogmas of Christianity must be accepted by the faithful. Doubt or denial leads to expulsion from the community. In popular usage dogma has acquired connotations of arrogance, authoritarianism and naked assertion. Mostly I will speak of dogma in the technical theological sense. The context will indicate where the term is being used in a wider and looser sense or with the overtones of ordinary speech.

Before setting out ways of interpreting dogmas positively, let us review the main lines of criticism. Are Christian dogmas a fundamental threat to human thought and liberty?

SOME TERMS USED OF THE MAGISTERIUM OR TEACHING OFFICE IN THE CATHOLIC CHURCH

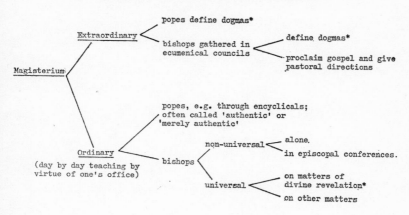

The ordinary, universal *magisterium* has been deemed to teach non-defined dogmas when: (1) the bishops throughout the world in union with the Bishop of Rome, (2) representing the whole Church and proclaiming the truth to the whole Church, (3) unanimously teach a matter of divine revelation as such to be held now and forever. To quote Vatican I: 'All those things are to be believed on divine and catholic faith, which are contained in the written or transmitted word of God and either by a solemn judgement or by the ordinary and universal *magisterium* are proposed for belief as having been divinely revealed' (DS 3011). Roman Catholic theology has recognized dogmas only at the asterisked points. Van Harvey misrepresents this theology when he explains that Roman Catholics 'regard all the pronouncements and creeds of all the councils up to the latest Second Vatican Council as having dogmatic status' (*A Handbook of Theological*

8

Terms [London, 1966] p. 63). The 'pronouncements of councils' extend far beyond dogmatic definitions. Vatican II offered no solemn definition of dogmatic status, but pronounced on a wide range of topics. It also summarised the teaching roles of pope and bishops in its Dogmatic Constitution on the Church (*Lumen Gentium*, par. 25).

II

The Case Against Dogma

I expect but little success of all this upon the *Dogmatist*,
his opinion'd assurance is paramont to Argument, and
'tis almost as easie to reason him out of a *Feaver*, as out of
this disease of the mind.

Joseph Glanvill, *The Vanity of Dogmatizing*

DOGMAS LOOK THOROUGHLY undesirable. Whether we take the
term in the narrower, theological sense or in the looser, popular
sense, we dare not bypass the strong case against dogmas. Christian and specifically Catholic dogmas have produced countless evil
effects. It would be outrageous if one were content to line up a
few half-hearted objections like straw men and play down the full
power of the counter-positions. Four words gather together much
of the case against dogmatic Christianity: liberty, reason, language and politics.

FREEDOM DENIED

First, dogma readily suggests a denial of liberty. It recalls endless violence done to the human conscience and ferocious persecutions of those who deviated from the norms of orthodoxy. Dogma
has a vicious face. Almost from the beginning of Christianity
Church authorities have mobilized physical and religious fear in
the service of compliance. In 385 the Spaniard Priscillian was
decapitated on the initiative of several bishops, who used charges

of sorcery and Manichaeism against him. His death in Trier puts Priscillian among the first of countless Christians, Jews and others to be executed under official Christian auspices. As Grand Inquisitor of Spain, Thomas de Torquemada (d. 1498) sent at least 2,000—perhaps even 10,000—Jews, apostates and other spiritual 'offenders' to the stake. In 1553 Michael Servetus was burned alive in Calvin's Geneva because he questioned the doctrine of the Trinity. From the other side of the reformation divide Pope Paul IV (1555–9) agreed that dogmatic deviation demanded eradication by such methods. 'Even if my own father were a heretic', he declared, 'I would gladly gather wood to have him burnt.' How could one even start to list the best-known victims of fanatical orthodoxy? Giordano Bruno, Edmund Campion, Thomas Cranmer, John Huss, John of Oldenbarneveldt, Oliver Plunkett—the names roll on endlessly paying hideous tribute to Christian man's readiness to take life in the cause of revealed truth. Recalling 'the fury of those *flames*' which dogmatic zeal had kindled, Joseph Glanvill reflected in the seventeenth century : ' 'tis lamentable that *Homo homini Daemon* should be a *Proverb* among the Professors of the *Cross*, and yet I fear it is as verifiable among them, as of those without the pale of visible *Christianity.*'[1] Avery Dulles understates heavily when he refers to the pyrotechnics of dogmatic definition and anathematization'. 'Erring Christians', he explains, 'were accused of being proud, stubborn, and shameless in their adulteration of the word of God and were threatened with eternal penalties if they failed to submit.' Would that it only went so far! Often severe penalties in this life posed a much more immediate threat than any penalties in the next life. A passing reference by Dulles to the Church's 'harshness toward adversaries' hardly does justice to an outrageous history of religious persecution.[2]

Doubtless some readers will feel that it is poor taste to rake up past offences and tediously recall once again how Catholics and Protestants, Spaniards and Germans, Englishmen and Frenchmen have committed ruthless murders in the name of orthodox be-

lief. If we flatter ourselves that our bloody past is really over,
what has happened in the twentieth century? For the sake of
revealed truth Christians have continued to rob their fellow-
Christians and others of freedom in what they say, write and do.
Preachers have been banned, writers silenced and teachers depri-
ved of their posts. Where once an anathema could lead to im-
prisonment and death, today it can bring exclusion from Church
membership. Economic sanctions, social penalties and charges of
self-indulgent trendiness have replaced burning at the stake.
Attempts to manipulate what Christians think and believe go
much further, of course, than merely silencing doubt, criticism
and protest. They include much indoctrination, one might call it
'indogmatization', which has masqueraded as religious educa-
tion. These are the systems which imprison 'the minds of the
young in a rigid armour of dogma'.³

A self-imposed denial of freedom has sometimes been as much
at work as external coercion. The sincere desire to remain loyal
has motivated many Catholics in their struggle to grapple with
and submit obediently to traditional formulations. Even where
they could scarcely understand, let alone really believe, what
some dogma meant, they were willing to accept it. The value of
belonging to the community overrode other considerations and
made them ready to sacrifice their intellects. For centuries Church
councils and popes have gone on piling up dogmas like a great
compost heap which twentieth-century Catholics inherit from the
past. Dogmatic development has been seen not only as never-
ending but also as irreversibly cumulative. Official claims that
dogmas are irrevocable rule out the instinct for de-development
and demolition. Surely some dogmas may have been malforma-
tions? Must all growth be self-authenticating? The loyal Catholic
theologian appears desperately burdened with the weight of a
dogmatic heritage, which he attempts to support but which threa-
tens to crush him. What does he achieve by his endless efforts
to resuscitate, explain and defend the dogmas of his Church?
This inheritance ties his hands in his pursuit of dialogue with

other Christians and with those of other faiths. How can he cope with the dogmas of the immaculate conception and the assumption in working towards reunion? Seemingly he remains so bound that he must simply wait until others see their way clear to accepting these Marian dogmas.

Finally, not just the history but the very notion of Christian dogma can strike us as incompatible with human freedom. Prescribed formulations rule out free, personal faith. When the appropriate authorities proclaim a truth as 'binding on all the faithful', what are the faithful bound to? Are they required merely to recite a set of words, or at least not to question and deny publicly this set of words? That sounds like sheer formalism, an extrinsic observance alien to true Christianity. St Paul reminds his Roman readers that they must not only 'confess with their lips' but also 'believe with their hearts' the gospel message (Rom 10 : 8–10). Can we reduce dogmas to the status of public regulations controlling Christian discourse? Dogmas would then become no more than language laws encouraging believers to use certain words (*homoousios*, transubstantiation, papal infallibility and so forth), and refrain from using other words (*homoiousios*, consubstantiation, papal fallibility and so forth). A heretic would then be not a man who believes what is false, but one who rejects such language controls and talks in a different way from the official language of Christians. He puts himself outside their linguistic community, because he claims the right to express his religious experience in words of his own choosing.

Or does the 'binding' nature of dogma reach beyond language laws to touch inner convictions? Are the faithful *obliged* to internalize formulations—to accept with their minds and believe interiorly what dogmas mean? We may want to challenge both the morality and the possibility of compelling interior assent by external commands. Can and should Church authorities instruct those faithful who are doubtful about a new dogma not merely to change their words but to change their minds? Such an injunction implies the questionable view that we are just as responsible for our beliefs as for our language and our behaviour.

To sum up. In the technical definition of dogma the phrase 'binding on all the faithful' either says too little or it says too much. It says too little, if it concerns no more than external regulations of language. It says too much, if it implies that dogmas can and should exercise a normative control over the inner beliefs of both Christians in general and Church leaders and teachers in particular. But in both cases liberty is threatened. In the first case free development of religious speech is impeded. In the second case a degree of responsibility for personal beliefs is implied which fails to correspond to much experience.

A second set of arguments against Christian dogmas, which cluster under the word 'reason', can run in opposite directions. On the one hand, dogmas appear irrational. On the other hand, they imply an intellectualism foreign to Jesus' gospel and the main thrust of the New Testament message. Let me develop these two points.

ARE DOGMAS IRRATIONAL?

Contrasting 'dogma' with 'an attitude of scientific inquiry',[4] Bertrand Russell argues that the virtue of 'truthfulness or intellectual integrity' is 'more likely to be found among those who reject religious dogmas than among those who accept them'. 'This virtue', he adds, 'is underestimated by almost all adherents of any system of dogma.'[5] The age of enlightenment has long ago come. But many Christians continue to exempt their cherished dogmas from rational scrutiny and historical criticism. Lloyd Geering spoke for himself rather than many of his fellow-Christians when he observed: 'The age of dogma is over and all inquiries must be pursued with openness.'[6] Dogma connotes a lack of openness and an adherence to rigid systems. It denies the dignity of an enlightened man to submit only to what he has critically examined and accepted on appropriate grounds.

Critics have scorned Christians for their willingness to renounce reason and accept dogma in the spirit of *credo quia absurdum.*

Karl Barth boldly made a virtue of this irrationality when he wrote in his classic commentary on Romans : 'All the articles of our Christian belief are, when considered rationally, impossible and mendacious and preposterous. Faith, however, is completely abreast of the situation. It grips reason by the throat and strangles the beast.'[7] This dogmatic assassination of reason prompted Dietrich Bonhoeffer to stigmatize Barth's view as a 'positivist doctrine of revelation which says in effect, "Like it or lump it" '.[8]

Very often the irrational insistence on dogma shows itself in the refusal to look honestly at the data of history. Long ago Vincent of Lerins enunciated his canon of Catholicity : 'One must take the greatest possible care to believe what has been believed everywhere, ever, by everyone.'[9] This principle suggests that innovation is automatically heretical. It asserts that the history of orthodox belief must be both devoid of change and transcultural. Too often a Vincentian presupposition ruled out in principle conclusions which believers were unwilling to reach through historical research. It has taken a long time for the recognition to be allowed to grow that dogmas may enshrine not sacrosanct truths of revelation, but theological opinions which won the day. George Vass writes :

> Theological opinions have been raised solemnly to the status of the dogmatic teaching of the church . . . positions like those of the Athanasian consubstantiality, or the medieval theory of grace as an infused habit, or the eucharistic presence as the result of a transubstantiating sacramental activity *did* establish themselves as *the* dogmatic teaching of the church.[10]

Even now this mild historical observation would not be accepted 'everywhere and by everyone'. The need for religious security partly accounts for such stubborn and uncritical reverence for dogmas. This is to explain, but not to excuse, stunning and persistent refusals to allow historical and rational evidence to question the status of dogmas.

ARE DOGMAS TOO RATIONAL?

The objections to dogmas, however, have frequently run in a direction roughly opposite to one taken by Bertrand Russell and others. It is the very intellectual and philosophical quality of dogmas that comes under fire. High-sounding formulations about Christ's one person in two natures (Council of Chalcedon) or about the kinds of causality involved in the sacraments (Council of Trent) may contain venerable and interesting ideas. But they have become so far removed from the original good news that they hinder and conceal faith rather than facilitate and reveal it. They have entangled the gospel of salvation in rationalism. Jesus did not teach abstract dogmas, but spoke in a concrete fashion through parables. He called on his hearers to make an unconditional surrender to his Father and believe in the glad tidings of God's coming kingdom. His invitation to them ran : 'Follow me, confess me before men.' He revealed not a system of dogmas to be understood, but a discipleship to be accepted. His truth was not a new set of doctrinal formulations, but a way of life (Jn 14 : 6). Before admitting men and women as his followers, he did not require of them the kind of oral and written professions of orthodoxy that have been required in the Catholic Church from bishops and professors of theology before they assumed office. Rather he asked for radical faith, love and personal adherence. Three centuries ago Glanvill asked :

> If our Returning Lord shall scarse find *faith* on earth, where will he look for *charity*? . . . What a stir is there for *Mint*, *Anise*, and *Cummin controversies*. while the great practical fundamentals are unstudyed, unobserved? What eagerness in the prosecution of *disciplinarian* uncertainties, when the love of God and our neighbour, those Evangelical *unquestionables*, want that fervent ardor?[11]

Have dogmas replaced 'believing in' Christ with 'believing that' certain truths are the case? Has the *fides quae* (the faith which is believed) crowded out the *fides qua* (the faith by which we commit ourselves)? In this context Thomas Aquinas has been quoted a thousand times already, but one more time will not hurt: '*Actus . . . credentis non terminatur ad enuntiabile, sed ad rem* (the act of believing does not terminate at what can be enunciated, but at the thing).'[12] Surely dogmas suggest that the act of faith stops at the propositions of revealed truth, but not at the 'thing' itself, the person of Jesus Christ?

In the light of the first Good Friday and Easter Sunday St Paul developed Jesus' call to faith. Believing in a list of dogmas would have struck the apostle as a return to law, an attempt at self-justification through the works of the intellect. Only personal faith in Christ crucified and risen saves, not an orthodox profession of objective truths. A dogmatic Christianity substitutes the dead letter for the living Spirit. In their *Geography of Faith* Robert Coles and Daniel Berrigan pressed each other as to where their religious commitment had led them to take their stand.[13] We would have been surprised to find the book entitled *Geography of Dogma*. Real faith sets men and women on the side of peace, healing and justice. The geography of dogma has too often caused them to stand for divisiveness, destruction and oppression. The Christianity of practical deeds, espoused by Leo Tolstoy and Albert Schweitzer, challenges all those dogmatic systems which ignore the claims of love. Does reluctance to believe a large set of dogmatic formulas exclude deep engagement as Christ's disciple? Many friends of his message of love have shown themselves enemies of dogma. Many friends of dogma have shown themselves the enemies of this love. The Old and New Testament books converge with what we know of Christ's own proclamation by dealing in personal categories and confronting men with God's saving action. Dogmas seem to evade the deepest issues of personal relationships by piling up ontological concepts and offering us doctrinal norms.

FALSE HELLENIZATION

A popular thesis about the hellenization of Christianity has often expressed this line of objection. One can name Adolf Harnack, Rudolf Bultmann, Leslie Dewart and Adolf Holl among those who have contrasted the original purity of the gospel with the secondary, ontological language of dogmas which grew under the influence of hellenic culture. Harnack noted the invasion of Greek intellectualism and concluded that dogma 'in its conception and its development' was nothing else but 'a work of Greek spirit on the soil of the gospel'. In particular the *Logos* doctrine legitimated Greek philosophical speculation within the life of the Church.[14] Christian faith came to be combined with and to depend upon an alien and highly metaphysical philosophy. Bultmann remained loyal to Harnack by criticizing the World Council of Churches' Christological confession. It rested on the Council of Chalcedon and 'the tradition of Greek thought' which focused reflection in 'the ancient Church'. He wrote :

> The New Testament indeed holds unmistakenly fast to the humanity of Jesus over against all gnostic doctrine, naturally with a naiveté for which the problems of 'very God and very man' have not yet arisen—those problems which the ancient Church doubtless saw, but sought to solve in an inadequate way by means of Greek thought with its objectivizing nature; a solution which indeed found an expression that is now impossible for our thought, in the Chalcedonian formula.[15]

Where Harnack took the process of hellenization as a dogmatic corruption, Dewart interprets it as a stage of development which was once useful but now proves no longer relevant.[16] He explicitly dissociates his interpretation of hellenism from that of Harnack.[17] Nevertheless, he calls on his readers to transcend their Greek past. Only thus can they be faithful both to the gospel message and to the demands of the future. Holl handles the development of dogma in the post-apostolic period more severely. It meant a shift away from the historical Jesus to a Christ who was both dogmatic *and dangerous*. 'The fundamental dogmas of the divine sonship of Jesus' represented not only the typical deification of the founder of a religion but also a degeneration into anti-Semitism.

> Deification . . . is a process in which the mass of believers subject themselves totally to the glorified Christ but . . . without identifying with him. Any remaining feelings of aggression towards this deified figure are transferred to the Jews. In this process Jesus the man, the Jew, is pushed out of mind, forgotten. Through deification and anti-Semitism Christendom has largely disburdened itself of the task of following Jesus.[18]

Holl gives a fresh twist to Harnack's basic thesis by introducing social psychology and Max Scheler's reflections on the deification of religious founders. The moral is essentially the same. We must strip away the later overlay of dogmas to allow the original message of Jesus to shine through again in its essential beauty.

DOGMAS AND LANGUAGE

In the third place, a case against dogma may raise objections for reasons of *language*. Dogmas claim not only to express the mystery of God's revelation in Christ, but also to lay down formulations valid for ever. In its dogmatic teaching on the sacraments the Council of Trent showed a typically sixteenth-century confidence in the power of words to express ultimate reality. These detailed assertions about the way sacraments work conflict with a proper recognition of God's incomprehensibility. How can anyone offer such lengthy descriptions of the way the divine grace reaches us, and still admit that the most important thing we know about God's being and actions is that we fail to know anything about them at all? By venturing to 'define' some revealed doctrine, councils and popes seemingly commit themselves to set out in precise words, and fix linguistic boundaries for, some aspect of God's mysterious dealings with mankind.

Moreover, permanently valid definitions appear to claim access to canonized, trans-temporal language. What justifies anyone in asserting that he speaks a perennial language to enshrine perennial truths? Is it possible to rise above historical relativities and articulate faith in such timeless formulations? Many of us have become nauseated by the current language of the mass media with its maximal impact and instant obsolescence. Nevertheless, this media language does forcibly remind us how changing and contingent all language is. How then can any dogma imprison some aspect of revelation in a definitive formula, which could be imposed upon men of all times and places? And yet defenders of dogmas have claimed to freeze revelation in expressions that will be valid always and everywhere. Is it plausible to make dogmatic formulations such a unique exception to the general mutability of human language?

What in fact has frequently happened is that believers have kept the old words but substituted new meanings. 'The dogmas of the Church', George Tyrrell remarked, 'change their sense, if not necessarily their expression, with the ages to which they are addressed.'[19] The terminology may remain, but not as perennial language enshrining the *same* perennial truths. Christian believers often stubbornly retain traditional formulas, when in fact the original beliefs which those formulas were intended to express are no longer there. Thus the consecrated language denying salvation outside the Church (*extra ecclesiam nulla salus*) has persisted through the centuries but with drastic changes of meaning. What the Fourth Lateran Council of 1215 (DS 802) and Boniface VIII in his bull *Unam Sanctam* of 1302 (DS 870–75) understood by this language differed sharply from the interpretation of Vatican II in its *Constitution on the Church (Lumen Gentium)*.[20] Not only the interpretation of 'the Church' has changed but also the meaning of 'outside'. A general willingness to obey God can be reckoned an implicit desire to belong to the Church which brings one 'inside'. Transubstantiation is another classic example of keeping the words but changing the meaning.

The Fourth Lateran Council (DS 802) used this term to express the Eucharistic presence of Christ under the appearance of bread and wine. Thomas Aquinas had not yet elaborated his sacramental doctrine on Aristotelian principles. Later the Council of Trent inevitably reflected Thomist theology in its teaching on transubstantiation (DS 1651ff.). To create an impression of secure continuity language may be artificially canonized, but shifts of meaning will occur.

DOGMAS AND POLITICS

'Politics' forms the fourth and last heading which gathers together many arguments against Christian dogmas. Should we unmask dogmas as no more than oblique statements about the political and social order? Are they, like ritual actions, no more than forms of symbolic statements about society? The cultural derivation and ideological motivation of dogmas call for close scrutiny. They may serve the needs of various ethnic and cultural groups. How much of Vatican I was an exercise of power-play by the Italian Church? Ecclesiastical rivalries, personal ambitions and the naked desire to curry favour with rulers could lie behind the proclamation of some dogmas. Surely we unmask the 'real' nature of dogmatic formulations by asking: What were their political causes and implications? Whose self-interests did they serve? *Cui bono*? Karl Marx saw 'the criticism of heaven' being 'transformed into the criticism of earth, the criticism of religion into the criticism of law, and the criticism of theology into the criticism of politics'.[21] The ultimate objection to dogma is not that they misrepresent Jesus' gospel, threaten human freedom and substitute naked authoritarianism for the exercise of human freedom. The case against dogma needs to move beyond theology and religion to politics and ideology.

One could instance the part Roman emperors played in the Christological dogmas which developed through the fourth and fifth centuries. The empire required a unified religious ideology, which both reflected and preserved patterns of social dominance.

A Church divided over fundamental beliefs was intolerable for the harmonious running of the state. Constantine set the pattern for his successors by summoning the Council of Nicaea (325) to secure agreement over Christ's relation to God the Father. He hoped for a basic religious harmony which could help to unify the Roman Empire. A Christianity liberated from persecution took over rapidly the task of the old pagan beliefs. We need to unmask in the Nicene Creed the political function which predominated over any stake in question of revealed truth. Eventually Justinian used the Chalcedonian confession as a law to maintain the necessary social consensus. Dogmas provided the ideological basis for the civil code. The later principle *cuius regio eius religio* could have read: *Cuius regio eius dogmata.* Political geography both determined and depended upon its own dogmas. Since the fourth century the throne has repeatedly spoken at the altar or from the pulpit. Marian dogmas provide a recent example. *The New Statesman and Nation* interpreted Pius XII's definition of Mary's assumption as serving to manipulate the faithful, shield them against the appeal of Marxism and keep them in economic and political subjection.

> As a correspondent from Rome puts it: 'It is stressed by a Catholic observer here that every dogma proclaimed tends to increase religious feeling among the masses.' If it increases religious feeling, it decreases the threat of material revolution . . . The Papal hierarchy is . . . well accustomed to a system in which the masses hunger while the landlords and capitalists contribute to the Church funds.[22]

Two hundred years ago Paul Thiry d'Holbach denounced just as vigorously such dogmatic bondage as an 'error', which serves the interests of the dominant classes in an unjust society and has cost mankind 'numberless calamities'.

> It is to error that must be attributed those insupportable chains which tyrants and priests have forged for all nations. It is to

error that must be attributed that slavery which the people of almost every country have fallen into . . . It is to error that must be attributed those inveterate hatreds, those barbarous presecutions, those continual massacres, and those dreadful tragedies of which the earth has too often been made the theatre, under pretence of serving the interests of heaven.[23]

Is dogma no more than a mask for such political and religious tyranny, a tool used to block human freedom and happiness?

I hope that the four sections of this chapter have presented with some fairness the main lines of attack on dogma. These counter-positions recall outrageously evil effects which were undeniably connected with Christian dogmas. Was that misery not accidental or incidental but the direct and proper consequence of dogmatic Christianity? In brief, is the pathology essential to dogma? Or can we repudiate the deadly use of dogma as no more than crimes perpetrated by wicked and misguided men? Is it possible to understand dogma in a humanly credible way? To these questions we turn in the following chapter.

III

Functions of Dogma

The dogmas of religion . . . do not have . . . only a practical sense, as expressing an intention to follow a policy of action, for although they do express something of the sort, this is inseparable from the conviction that such a policy is both demanded and supported by the structure of reality.

John Macquarrie, *Principles of Theology*

A dogmatic statement . . . intends a definite objective content which has its own existence opposite the speaker —it is not merely the publication of a subjective state of the speaker.

Karl Rahner, *Theological Investigations*

CAN DOGMAS FUNCTION in a healthy fashion? Or do they represent an essentially diseased development of Christianity which must be firmly excised? The previous chapter outlined a typical series of outraged objections to dogmas. In general it is true that anyone who has never become indignant with Christianity has never really known it. Specifically, if we have never felt anger at the development and use of Christian dogmas, can we qualify to examine the case for dogma? This chapter explores ways in which dogmas might work as guides and incentives to genuinely Christian living. Whether this account substantially fails to fit the facts of the two thousand years and remains an illusory ideal can be left for discussion in the next chapter. Our roles as listeners, speakers and members of the Church suggest three ways of approaching the positive effects of dogmas.

DESCRIPTION AND PRESCRIPTION

First of all, when we hear dogmas, we are being offered more than sheer information, certainly more than purely theoretical information, if such a thing exists. Dogmas enjoy a *prescriptive* function as well as a *descriptive* one. They make truth claims about the God who meets us in Christ, but in such a way as to prescribe some appropriate reaction to these saving truths. Like religious doctrines in general, dogmas purport not only to make sense of the world, but also to help us 'to formulate and apply policies of moral behaviour'.[1] Let us take two examples from the Chalcedonian definition and Trent's teaching on the sacraments.

The definition from Chalcedon begins :

> We all with one accord teach men to acknowledge one and the same Son, our Lord Jesus Christ, at once complete in Godhead and complete in manhood, truly God and truly man, consisting also of a reasonable soul and body; of one substance with the Father as regards his Godhead, and at the same time of one substance with us as regards his manhood; like us in all respects, apart from sin; as regards his Godhead, begotten of the Father before the ages, but yet as regards his manhood begotten, for us men and for our salvation, of Mary the Virgin, the God-bearer; one and the same Christ, Son, Lord, Only-begotten, recognized in two natures, without confusion, without change, without division, without separation; the distinction of natures being in no way annulled by the union, but rather the characteristics of each nature being preserved and coming together to form one person and subsistence.[2]

Antony Flew rightly insists that we must not ignore the cognitive intention of believers' assertions, and interpret their assertions as no more than 'crypto-commands, expressions of wishes, disguised ejaculations, concealed ethics'.[3] Nevertheless, the fathers at Chalcedon planned to do more than merely describe how, as a matter of fact, they understood the person of Jesus of Nazareth. They wished to direct their listeners to the mystery of the God become man, so that faith in Christ might be renewed and men brought into closer communion with him. The Council of Trent began its teaching on the sacraments by announcing :

> If anyone says that the sacraments of the New Law are not all instituted by Jesus Christ our Lord, or are more or fewer than seven (namely, baptism, confirmation, Eucharist, penance, extreme unction, orders and matrimony), or even that one of these seven is not truly and properly a sacrament, let him be anathema (DS 1601).

Here again the members of a Church council proclaim truth for the sake of salvation. They do not make their statements simply because they feel it to be their duty to make them, but without caring whether their audiences believes them or not. They report how they believe things to be, *with the intention* of regulating and renewing the lives of their audience. In effect they both announce, 'There are seven sacraments', and enjoin the faithful : 'Practise a full sacramental life.' The prescription is implicit in the description. Trent offers as much a guide to proper religious attitudes and Christian practice as an illumination for the mind. With both Chalcedon and Trent apparently straightforward statements ('Christ is one person in two natures' and 'Christ instituted seven sacraments') are used to do more than simply offer or recall information. This can, of course, happen in contexts which have nothing to do with the dogmatic formulations of Christians, as P. F. Strawson points out :

> There are many different circumstances in which the simple sentence-pattern 'X is Y' may be used to do things which are not merely stating (though they all involve stating) that X is Y. In uttering words of this simple pattern we may be encour-

aging, reproving, or warning someone; reminding someone; answering, or replying to, someone; denying what someone has said; confirming, granting, corroborating, agreeing with, admitting what someone has said. Which of these, if any, we are doing depends on the circumstances in which, using this simple sentence-pattern, we assert that X is Y.[4]

DISCERNMENT AND COMMITMENT

Besides reflecting on the situation of those who listen to dogmas, we need to examine the role of the *speaker*. Here also we fail to expound dogmas appropriately, unless we respect the complex nature of what takes place. One extreme takes the speaker to be merely expressing the view of a neutral observer. The other extreme maintains that he is simply conveying his intention to follow a certain course of action. But in fact both *discernment* and *commitment* are involved. The speaker not only reports what the believes to be the case about the world, but also testifies to his own personal act of faith. On the one hand, he discerns that such and such holds true about Christ's existence, the nature of the sacraments of the destiny of the Virgin Mary. His statements of belief are statements with an informative content. They maintain certain claims to objective truth. On the other hand, he also expresses his personal response in the face of this truth. If he points to the reality of Christ's divine origin, he also commits himself subjectively to appropriate decisions on the basis of this reality. He praises, worships and entrusts his life to the God-man. His discernment of the status of the seven sacraments entails a commitment to the requisite self-involvement in sacramental life.

Any interpretation of dogmas remains essentially impoverished, unless it attends to this connection between formulations of objective belief and subjective patterns of moral behaviour. What the speaker sees to be true he also holds to be valuable. The true is the good : *verum et bonum convertuntur*. Dogmas express a faith-attitude of the whole human self, an attitude of *both* acknowledgement *and* commitment in the face of divine revelation. The level of discernment and commitment can vary indefinitely. In Chapter VI we draw some consequences from this phenomenon.

We have looked at what hearing and uttering a dogma ideally involves. The words used (prescriptive and descriptive, discernment and commitment) share the weakness of being rather solemn, although perhaps we inevitably become somewhat solemn when we discuss the ways Christian dogmas work or fail to work. We do not always find the two elements equally present. At times prescription and commitment predominate. Dogmas may be directed more to guide conduct or pledge oneself to certain actions than to offer any description. For instance, the Council of Trent anathematized those who denied that 'in the three sacraments of baptism, confirmation and orders there was imprinted on the soul a character, that is to say, a spiritual and indelible sign' (DS 1609). The bishops at Trent wanted to preserve the orthodox practice of not administering these three sacraments again to anyone who had already received them. Their main aim was scarcely to describe the sacramental character.

TWO GENERALIZATIONS

If generalizations are not to be boring, they must be slightly risky. Let me offer two generalizations. First, with the fourth Lateran Council in 1215 dogmas tended to shift from being heavily admonitory and prescriptive to incorporate more descriptive elements. This generalization demands, nevertheless, qualification. On the one hand, earlier formulations did attempt descriptions. Constantinople III (A.D. 680–681) solemnly declared that in Christ there are 'two natural wills', a human will and a divine will (DS 556). On the other hand, Trent admonished its readers that 'the intention of doing at least what the Church does is required of ministers when they perform and confer the sacraments' (DS 1611). The council wished to ensure that this minimal intention accompany the celebration of the sacraments. The moral injunction was more important than any factual statement about the way the minister's intention actually worked.

Second, both in earlier and later Church history dogmas have proved much more successful at guiding conduct, warning the faithful against aberrations and promising lines of commitment than at giving objective accounts of anything. Often they have been informative only in a vague and abstract way. At the heart of the Chalcedonian confession four negatives balance each other carefully – 'without confusion, without change, without division, without separation'. Even if dogmas may be called descriptive, they hardly seek to explain anything, let alone explain it completely. Believers have not enjoyed notable success at interpreting their experience with the help simply of dogmas. However we judge Trent's formulations on the sacraments (DS 1601ff.), they fail to explain to us at depth what sharing in the sacramental life is like.

It would be difficult to sustain the case that dogmas are primarily informative. Do Christians *know* more of the divine reality after hearing a dogma for the first time? Dogmas are not normally fresh pieces of information confronting our inner vision like new photographs. They tend to clarify something or remind us of some truth rather than offer some information for the first time. Faced with a situation of controversy, the Council of Chalcedon authoritatively decided in favour of certain terms for describing Christ's existence. That council did not present fifth-century Christians with vital pieces of information about Christ which had remained hitherto unavailable. The Council of Trent insisted on retaining seven sacraments, clarified the nature of justification, laid down the canon of scriptures, and in general severely warned the faithful against what it took to be the aberrations of the reformers. It offered precise reminders, pastoral directions and terminological decisions much more than informative descriptions.

So far from regretting that dogmatic pronouncements have served primarily to guide conduct, we might wish that they had enjoyed even greater success in that direction. What I have in mind is this. At many levels dogmas have levelled criticism at secular realities, a criticism which should have led to revolutionary practice. Frequently Christians have failed to draw the social and political consequences for their conduct. Let us take two examples. Chalcedon acknowledged Christ as being 'of one substance with us as regards his manhood'. This confession radically opposed the institution of slavery, which in effect denied that Christ shared a human nature with *all* of us. Christians took well over a thousand years to draw this consequence in practice. We can cite also the definition of Mary's immaculate conception from 1854. The belief that (through her being preserved even from original sin) a woman ranks as the most perfectly redeemed human person carried implications about attitudes towards women in the life of the Church. How could all those men who believed this of Mary have continued to treat women as second-class Christians and second-class human beings? Bishops and priests have dominated institutes of nuns, kept the ordained ministry as an exclusively male preserve and generally behaved as if, through their wisdom and strength, they enjoyed a privileged position in the matter of redemption. Not just the 1854 definition but traditional Marian devotion should have transformed treatment of women. Beliefs about Mary radically conflict with the stunning and persistent refusal to allow genuine equality, freedom and justice for women. True critical insight into the Chalcedonian confession and the dogma of the immaculate conception would have uncovered unsuspected responsibilities to alter society and further the cause of human liberation.

TENSION BETWEEN DESCRIPTION AND PRESCRIPTION

Two final points call for attention before we leave (1) the prescriptive and descriptive elements involved in hearing dogmas, and (2) the discernment and commitment involved in uttering dogmas. Tension may arise between the descriptive and the prescriptive elements. The dogmatic canons of Trent worked effectively to guide conduct and secure consensus within the Roman Catholic Church, but notoriously some of the council's descriptions (for instance, of original sin) have called for radical reassessment. The later Church upheld the insight which the Council of Nicaea expressed by describing Christ as *homoousios* (of one substance) with the Father. Nevertheless, at least in the short term the description failed to win universal acceptance. The Arian controversy dragged on through the fourth century. A given dogma could incorporate deep insights, but prove ineffective. Or it could prove effective in encouraging worship and discipleship, but convey little enlightenment about revelation.

Let me put my point in an extreme and unqualified fashion. We could find ourselves saying : 'This dogma is true, but doesn't work.' Or : 'This dogma works, but isn't true.' Karl Rahner touches on this tension between (1) description and discernment and (2) prescription and commitment, when he asks : 'Cannot even a truth be dangerous, equivocal, seductive, forward – can it not manoeuvre a person into a position where he must make a decision for which he is not fitted?'[5] The moral to be drawn is this. An obligation rests on Church leaders, if ever they are faced with the need to issue dogmatic pronouncements, to prove themselves *both* faithful to the truth of God's revelation *and* to their pastoral responsibilities. They must not sacrifice *either* their insights into truth *or* their duty to guide conduct. To put this negatively, they should be neither dishonest nor damaging.

If a tension exists between (1) the elements of commitment and prescription and (2) the elements of discernment and description, we can observe also a mutual influence. Commitment to Christ within the Church's life preceded the conscious clarification of what the Church believed and wished to say about his relationship to the Father. The celebration of the Eucharist had continued for more than a thousand years before Lateran IV (1215), the Council of Florence (1438–45) and the Council of Trent progressively pronounced on the nature of the Eucharistic sacrament and sacrifice. Century-long practice preceded elaborated theory. Only a resolute ignorance of history could allow anyone to suppose that the dogmas of Nicaea and the later councils formed some absolute starting-point, from which and according to which the Church could proceed for the first time to organize and direct its worship of Christ, its sacramental activity and the rest of its life. Nevertheless, discernment can provide commitment with greater self-awareness, which will support stronger and more lasting programmes of action. In turn transformed practice can influence theoretical descriptions. At every level living faith and formulations of belief enjoy a mutual impact.

DOGMA AND CHURCH

We have chewed over and picked apart what happens, or at least ideally happens when we hear or utter a dogma. This listening and speaking takes place within the Christian community. Neither as Christians nor as human beings can we acquire truth in individual isolation. Truth comes only through fellowship with other men and women. We first find God's word to us, deepen our understanding of it and grow as Christians through the community of believers. This community speaks to us through dogmas, as well as through sermons, liturgical prayers, creeds, the teaching of saints, catechisms and all the other forms which the written or spoken word of faith takes. It is high time to turn to the churchly character of dogmatic formulations. Three items need to be noted here. Dogmas offer linguistic rulings, are closely related to community creeds and evoke through analogy shared insight into divine revelation.

First, the Christological formulas from the fourth and fifth centuries clearly illustrate how dogmas function to offer *community rulings on terminology*. The decisions at the Councils of Nicaea, Constantinople I, Ephesus and Chalcedon aimed at creating and safeguarding unity through adopting common and clear expressions. This solidarity of belief in Christ drew lines against misleading terminology and helped to identify those who belonged to the community. Prayer, liturgy and preaching remained the primary language of the Church. Nourished by the scripture, this language must always continue to convey the real substance of genuinely Christian belief. As second-level propositions dogmas were introduced to guide the use of that primary religious language.

Through the role which they played at baptism and the Eucharist, creeds loomed large in that primary language. For our purposes it should be observed that credal structures combined (a) prayers of praise directed towards God with (b) teaching and witness addressed to men. In more technical terms, doxological utterances were blended with didactic formulas. Creeds like the Apostles Creed and the Niceno-Constantinopolitan Creed differed from later dogmas in several ways. They were used in liturgies, they rehearsed the whole plan of God's salvation from creation to the last judgement, and—despite the presence of words like *homoousios*—they adopted less philosophical language than many dogmas. Up to the beginning of the fourth century creeds were local and expressed the faith of particular churches rather than of the universal Church. Even later the names of Nicaea, Constantinople and Chalcedon preserved the original local flavour of creeds. Where once creeds clarified and summarized the gospel in particular historical circumstances and for the worship of particular communities, they came to serve as interpretative bulwarks against heresy. The shifts from the Niceno-Constantinopolitan Creed ('We believe') to Chalcedon ('We teach that it ought to be confessed') illustrates how liturgical confession gave way to doctrine about correct confession. The Chalcedon definition was not incorporated in the liturgy. The Athanasian Creed moved even further from worshipful praise as well as from positive witness to God's saving activity. It piled up dogmatic definitions against erroneous doctrines.

The change in creeds away from doxological and didactic functions in local liturgies allowed dogmatic formulations to emerge. Nevertheless, something of the original twofold structure of community creeds still characterizes dogmas. They remain doxological and didactic. Even such a prosaic-sounding dogma as the Tridentine definition of seven sacraments, which we quoted above, evokes praise (for the God who enriches us sacramentally) and testifies to the truth. We respond to dogmas appropriately when we recognize their elements of prayer and teaching. They both express wonder at some facet of divine redemption and bear witness to this.

DOGMA AND ANALOGY

Third, within the life of the Church dogmas evoke through *analogy* shared insight into divine revelation. Let us discuss in turn the role of analogies and their power to evoke faith. Like all theological and inter-personal language, dogmatic formulas deal in analogies. They constantly, if implicitly, express comparisons when they speak of the divine reality and man's status in the presence of God. Chalcedon introduces such terms as nature, person, manhood and Godhead. Trent talked of sacraments, sin, justification and so forth. Here theological language closely resembles the language of personal relations which must speak analogically when it speaks of love, trust, betrayal, faith and so on. Love can be passionate love, the love found in platonic friendships, love between siblings, love for one's country, love for one's work. We can imagine numerous relationships which, though extremely different, still show a sufficient resemblance to allow us to talk of love in each case.

Often the analogical quality of dogmatic language has either been quietly bypassed or extraordinarily misrepresented. M. E. Williams, for instance, writes as follows in an article on the nature of dogma :

Revelation is about unseen realities that transcend man's experience so that, by the nature of things, no language is adequate to express divine truth completely, and one must always fall back on analogy . . . That is why the pronouncements of the Church have always to be read in the context of their age.[6]

This statement houses several unacceptable convictions. First, human language frequently proves inadequate to express *completely* the reality of much that neither transcends man's experience nor is unseen. How can anyone express completely the reality of Rembrandt's masterpieces? What lover would agree that even the finest account exhausts the truth about the object of his love? He or she remains far more than the sum of any or all descriptions. Second, we should count and bury the false implications in the view that 'one must always fall back on analogy'. How regrettable it is that we cannot express the divine reality in abstract, mathematical language! The shades of Cartesian rationalism are lurking in the wings of this statement. Must we pity the poor theologians, art critics, historians, poets, dramatists and novelists who have to 'fall back' on analogies, instead of using clear, distinct and utterly univocal concepts? Their language lacks the precision of scientific language, but it is surely much more expressive. Third, admittedly some knowledge of the context of any particular age will be required to understand specific analogies. But this context extends to the contemporary questions, controversies and pastoral needs. The appearance of contemporary analogies suggests only one reason among many for reading dogmas in the context of their age.

To come back to the role of analogy in dogmas. Whatever one might maintain about other kinds of discourse, *precise* analogies are impossible in the field of religion, specifically when we seek to express revealed truth. An inevitable vagueness and imprecision always rule out attempts to settle finally questions of exact meaning and fixed truth. When we speak of God or Christ being 'at work' in the sacraments, we acknowledge that the divine work is something like, but definitely not the same as, any kind of human work. Our analogies fall somewhere along the scale between being totally different (an agnostic approach) and totally the same (an anthropomorphic approach). 'Somewhere' could be misleading. In fact these analogies cluster close to the extreme of sheer agnosticism. Every positive statement about God calls for a corresponding negative, as well as for the recognition that God transcends any attempts to catch his being and nature in a net of words. Our language about God is 'yes-but' language. *Yes*, God works through the sacraments (*via affirmationis*), *but* not as men and women work (*via negationis*). Always he works in ways that transcend our insights and language (*via eminentiae*).

Why should anyone bother to insist on this imprecision which dogmatic formulations share with religious language in general? My primary reason is distress at seeing that even valuable writers can apparently forget that precise analogies are ruled out in dogmatic discourse. The word 'definition' can lead them astray with its connotations of exactness. Thus Pelikan writes :

> Conciliar and creedal definitions may be called precise only in the sense that they draw the lines of the perimeter beyond which devotion and speculations may not go without violating orthodoxy. Within the perimeter, however, there remains, if not an agreement to disagree, at least a great deal of room for further speculations, debate, and perhaps dogmatic development. But in the case of many doctrines, there has been little or no delineation of such perimeters.[7]

Even this restricted use of 'precise' misleadingly suggests that dogmas delineate perimeters. What exact lines are drawn by describing Christ as one person in two natures? Can anyone pin down precisely what is meant by 'person', whether we attend to the usage of the fifth century or other centuries? After we have affirmed something positive, we will *both* deny that Christ is a person in the sense(s) in which we speak of our contemporaries as persons, *and* admit that his personhood eludes our grasp. Respect for the *via negationis* and the *via eminentiae* prevents us doing anything as clear-cut as delineating perimeters by our Christological definitions.

The analogies which dogmas incorporate are not only imprecise in themselves, but also evoke very different reactions. The use of any analogy always relies on the experience of readers and hearers. Where Church dogmas speak of salvation, justification from sin and the manhood of Christ, they depend on their audience having already experienced reality in ways which allow these terms to convey meaning. Communication will fail with those who have no sense of sin and lostness, or whose notions of what it is to be a man differ widely from that presupposed by a given dogmatic formulation. Prior experience of what the analogies are concerned with allows dogmas not only to convey meaning but also create moods, evoke various emotional reactions and frequently to communicate more by their richer connotations than by their vaguer denotations. A dogma's oblique implications for life may turn out to be more important for an individual than anything it directly denotes.

When Pius XII solemnly defined that the Virgin Mary at the end of her earthly existence had been assumed body and soul into heaven, this dogma evoked from some believers a renewed sense of Mary's maternal protection. The specific import of the pope's statement mattered less to them than their general desire to honour Christ's mother and revive a comforting sense of her loving concern. For others the dogma protested satisfyingly against degrading treatment of the human body, the unjust position of women and the oppression of mankind through death. Yet others heard Pius' proclamation precisely in terms of the meaning which their insights and experience helped them to find in the key words : assumption, body and soul, heaven.

What hangs upon the fact that the analogies used in dogmatic formulations rely upon the experience of their audience? Just this. Dogmas cannot affect their audiences along pre-defined lines. To the extent that they are prescriptive and enjoin certain forms of public commitment, they can enjoy some uniform effects. Trent's dogmatic teaching on the sacraments ensured that the Catholic Church retained the practice of seven sacraments. Insofar as they attempt to describe facets of divine revelation, however, dogmas will inevitably convey different things to different people. The various ways we have experienced reality and interpreted that experience will determine how we appreciate grace, salvation, personhood, sacraments, substance and the other analogous concepts which make up dogmas. We cannot come up with some standard list of experiences or fixed set of questions and answers, which everyone must bring to his reading of Chalcedon, Lateran IV, Trent and Vatican I. Influenced by inherited assumptions, personal experiences, individual decisions and our degrees of self-awareness, each of us has taken in a somewhat different world before we give these councils a hearing. The traditional axiom has its relevance here: *Quidquid recipitur per modum recipientis recipitur.* Dogmatic pronouncements by Church authorities cannot guarantee an identical reception by the community as a whole. Nor are they immune against leading hearers into mistakes and errors. If infallibility means 'immunity from error', it does *not* mean 'immunity against leading others into error'. The responses from the community will inevitably vary, because the analogies of religious language evoke different experiences from even the smallest audience of believers. Hence there is no such thing as *the* meaning of any given dogma. We return to this point in a later chapter where I discuss personal paraphrases.

To elucidate further my point about the reception of dogmatic definitions, it could help to compare the *public* and the *personal* spheres. On the public side Church councils or popes cannot predetermine what will happen to the words they use. Historical changes in language lie very largely beyond ecclesiastical control. Lateran IV described the central action of Eucharistic worship as transubstantiation, but could not lay down in advance that the denotations and connotations of that term were to remain unaltered, despite Thomas Aquinas, the Reformation, the Council of Trent and other usage, both theological and popular. All language has a public history. No Church council can adopt a Canute-like posture and fix lines over which linguistic change must never surge. On the personal side likewise, it lies beyond the competence of councils and popes to predetermine how their dogmatic definitions will be appropriated. The experiences of their audience remain endlessly various. In a rich and complex way the analogies of dogmatic language will appeal to (or fail to appeal to) the persons who hear those analogies.

If we recall that dogmas deal with *revealed* truth, it also becomes clear why they cannot affect their audience along fixed lines. Dogmatic formulas prove more or less successful not only at interpreting the foundational revelation in Christ which took place 'back there and then', but also at producing a situation of dependent revelation here and now. 'The dogmatic statement', Karl Rahner reflects, 'leads towards the historical event of salvation, in spite of all its conceptual reflection . . . It does not merely speak "about" this event but tries to bring man into a real relationship with it.'[8] Along with other forms of ecclesiastical teaching and proclamation, dogmas aim to create saving and revealing situations, through which God communicates himself and our faith is roused. But whether and how we hear God's claim and see his truth through any given dogma depends not only on his free gift, but also on the personal structure of our questions about the meaning of life. We never experience and express revelation 'neat', even when it is mediated by the most solemn dogmas of the Church. The interpretation and understanding which each of us brings to episodes in which God reveals himself partly determine what we make of these episodes.

This chapter has outlined ways in which dogmas *could* operate in a healthy fashion. It raised issues and took positions on some dogmas pronounced by councils and popes. It was simply not feasible to ask purely theoretical questions, while completely side-stepping the evaluation of any examples from the history of Christianity. Nevertheless, it seemed worth while trying first to get things straight about our interpretation of dogma as such. My aim was to create some basis for (a) discussing explicitly the actual limitations of dogmas, and (b) responding to the historical criticisms which we outlined in the previous chapter.

IV
Limiting and Defending Dogma

The root of dogma is the confession of Christ.
Edmund Schlink, *The Coming Christ and the Coming Church*

The care which the Church has always exercised in the
formulation of dogma, her fulminations against defective
or contrary formulations, have rested on the conviction
that the integrity of the images or symbols which domi-
nate a man's soul are of the utmost importance to his
own well-being, and that it is a matter of the highest
importance to him what he thinks and says about them.
Victor White, *Soul and Pysche*

WE CAN TACKLE dogmas (and related theological issues) in two
ways. On the one hand, we might accept them as a pre-given religious reality, brush off objections against them and disentangle
their essentially healthy function. In this case we would theo-
logize out of belief, assuming that the world of dogmas is not
wrong and seeking to adjust both our thinking and our conduct
to the order of dogmatic formulations. On the other hand, we
might dismiss this first approach as an improbable piece of ideal-
ism which denies concrete history and escapes into theoretical abstraction. No amount of reinterpretation can cover up the
inhumanly evil use of dogmas. In that case we would begin with
extreme dissatisfaction at this diseased development, convinced
that here Christianity was not as it ought to have been. We would
presume dogmas to be guilty until—or rather unless—someone

could perform the unexpected trick of proving them innocent.

The first approach offers sympathetic understanding; the second stresses the concrete evidence of history. I hope that Chapter III has responded fairly to the first approach and Chapter II to the second. My own problems with dogma which appear later in this book differ from the usual arguments raised by either side. Both approaches have in fact failed through their readiness to rip dogmas by a fishing-rod method from their lively and complex context in history. Many of the customary objections to, and exaggerated arguments for, dogma were possible, only because both opponents and defenders paid insufficient attention to the total structure of this context. The first side has been bent on maximising both the significance and the pathology of Church dogmas. The other side has also tended to maximize the value of dogmas while struggling to offer a satisfactory defence. In this chapter I plan to insist against the defenders of dogma that various limitations drastically diminish the value of dogmatic formulations, before reacting to objections from their opponents.

LIMITATIONS ON DOGMAS

The first limitation on the value of dogmas arises from the fact that we cannot treat them as ultimate norms for faith. Only the God who reveals himself in Christ is such a norm and object of faith. To give our ultimate and unconditional assent to dogmas as such would constitute an idolatrous act of worship that substituted formulas for the living God.

Moreover, the Christian Church has always recognized that no dogma can rise to the level of inspired scripture. All dogmas need to be checked against the record of foundational revelation which the bible provides. At some levels, of course, dogmas offer guidelines for the understanding of scripture. (1) They interpret particular biblical texts. Thus the Council of Trent insisted that John 20:22f. bore on the power to forgive sins in the sacrament of penance (DS 1703). (2) Dogmas reject specific interpretations of scripture. Trent outlawed the view which would explain metaphorically the *water* of (baptismal) regeneration in John 3:5 (DS 1615.) (3) Dogmas have singled out for special treatment a handful of biblical themes. Trent and previous councils dwelt on those few biblical scriptural passages which are recognizably concerned with the Eucharist and original sin. No council has solemnly defined the work of Christ, even though the New Testament abounds with material on the salvation effected through his life, death and resurrection. (4) Even though dogmatic formulations introduce terms like person, nature and infallibility, they also include in their vocabulary such scriptural concepts as sin, baptism, righteousness and sacrifice. This selection of certain biblical words and themes constitutes a form of interpretation. At a later stage dogmas look back to and interpret the bible. Nevertheless, in a much more significant way the scriptures, which belong to the very foundation of Christianity, interpret the dogmas of the later Church. In the light of the closed and complete canon of inspired scriptures we assess dogmatic formulations, which have grown through the history of Christianity and possibly will continue to appear. Ultimately, biblical statements are normative for dogmatic statements, not vice versa. The New Testament forms an *essential* part of the primal response (*Urantwort*) to the Christ-event. As a *contingent* element in the later responses, dogmas are radically relative to the scriptures.

Let me offer two examples. We judge Trent's teaching on transubstantiation in the light of the Last Supper narratives, not the other way round. The New Testament helps us to evaluate Marian dogmas. Both St Paul (Gal 4:4) and all four gospels witness to Mary as Christ's mother. Only Luke and Matthew introduce the virgin birth. No New Testament mentions Mary's assumption as such. The scriptures allow us to conclude that all Marian dogmas are equal but some are more equal than others. Her divine motherhood takes precedence over any dogmas concerned with the virgin birth or the assumption.

The scriptures are normative for dogmas. God's self-manifestation serves as the final criterion for faith. There should be no tampering with the order of value : divine revelation, scripture which records revelation and dogmas which later interpret revelation.[1] Tampering has often occurred not least through the theological 'notes' by which textbooks graded theological propositions : *de fide de finita certa, probabilis, de fide catholica* and so forth. This scale held a dogmatic definition from a council or pope to be the supreme criterion of certainty and security. So far as I know, *de fide biblica* never established itself as a theological 'note'. Yet in any scale of theological authority the scriptural record of foundational revelation and faith should have enjoyed precedence over later dogmatic formulations.

Some friendly interpretation is necessary, if we wish to find an acceptable meaning in the 1973 'Declaration in Defence of the Catholic Doctrine on the Church against certain errors of the present day' (*Mysterium Ecclesiae*) issued by the Sacred Congregation for the Doctrine of the Faith. The relevant passage reads : 'The objects of Catholic faith—which are called dogmas— necessarily are and always have been the unalterable norm both for faith and for theological science' (art. 3). We may call dogmas the proximate objects of and norm for faith, but never faith's ultimate Object and Norm, the God who drew near to us in Jesus Christ. Only God, not human language, can make absolute claims on us or provide ultimate guidelines for us. Moreover, the proximate norms for faith include preaching, liturgy and other elements in the Church's total life. Dogmas by no means monopolise the role of providing such proximate norms. 'Always' must be taken with a grain of salt. We would look in vain for anything like a defined dogma prior to the Council of Nicaea in 325.

Second, *the particularity of history* conditions and limits dogmatic formulations. They are cast in the language of a particular age in response to the particular questions and challenges of that age. Here *Mysterium Ecclesiae* proves more successful when it observes : 'The meaning of the pronouncements of faith depends partly upon the expressive power of the language used at a certain point in time and in particular circumstances' (art. 5). The particularity extends, of course, beyond language to a wide range of historical variables : current interpretations of scripture and tradition, contemporary theology and prevailing world-views (including views on the nature of man). The dogmatic pronouncements on revelation and faith issued by Vatican I provide a striking example. This council discloses a typically intellectualist bias of the nineteenth century which, despite its evident romantic and traditionalist elements, worshipped rational proof and revelled in the manufacture of vast systems of ideas. The pre-Freudian man of western Europe understood himself as a creature of clear intellect and noble will. Contemporary anthropology made its appearance as much as anything else when Vatican I confidently rehearsed the external 'arguments of revelation', the miracles and prophecies of both the Old and New Testaments, and pointed with pride to the convincing sign offered by the Church itself : 'The Church by itself, with its marvellous extension, its eminent holiness, and its inexhaustible fruitfulness in every good thing, with its Catholic unity and its invincible stability, is a great and perpetual motive of credibility and an irrefutable witness of its own divine mission' (DS 3009, 3013). A modification of nineteenth-century intellectual optimism would come later when the ambiguities, irrationalities and experimental nature of human existence received more adequate recognition— not to mention the discovery of the role of the unconscious.

No great difficulty exists for those who appreciate the anthropology of Vatican II and wish to introduce in this regard comparisons unfavourable to Vatican I. But we should not succumb to anachronism. In 1870 the work of Buber, Ebner, Freud, Heidegger, Camus, Sartre and Marcel still lay ahead—to say nothing of the revival of interest in Kierkegaard and many other forces working toward that richer grasp of human complexities on which North-Atlantic man prides himself. Furthermore, would Vatican I's account of revelation and faith have proved more successful in its own day, if the council had anticipated some personalist approaches of the twentieth century? Probably not. Such a miraculous anticipation of coming trends might, of course, have made Vatican I a greater aid and comfort to later Catholics than it has proved to be. But it is hardly fair play, unhampered by any statute of limitations, to put the bishops of Vatican I on trial a century later as if they were theological war criminals. With sympathy and honesty we must recognize in how many ways their particular context conditioned and limited their formulations.

If varying anthropological presuppositions are often passed over in silence, practically every writer on our subject notes one recurrent factor which renders dogmas particular. They are usually formulated when distortions threaten Christian belief. To put this point more concretely. Councils and popes normally directed their dogmatic formulations *against* certain heterodox positions. They felt the need to state revealed truths more precisely and so exclude particular errors. Pelikan rightly warns us that 'no conciliar or confessional promulgation can be properly understood apart from the anathemas it pronounces upon those who teach otherwise'.[2] A. N. Whitehead made the same observation but more concretely: 'Wherever there is a creed, there is a heretic round the corner or in his grave.'[3] Consequently dogmas are often more explicit in what they rule out than in what they affirm. The relation of the human and divine elements in Jesus Christ aroused lengthy controversy, which culminated in the classic dogmatic definition of Chalcedon. Four negatives nestled at the heart of this conciliar statement. The one person of Christ exists in two natures 'without confusion, without change, without division, without separation'. The council directed 'without confusion' against Eutychianism and 'without division' against Nestorianism. We can, however, easily exaggerate this claim that dogmas rule out more than they rule in. Chalcedon had positive information to convey in its description of Christ as one person in two natures. Even where error historically occasioned dogmatic pronouncements, these pronouncements often positively expressed Church teaching in a fuller way than was available before.

The error which a new dogma ruled out could have been held by persons long dead. Whitehead rightly noted that the heretic could be 'in his grave', as well as 'round the corner'. Thus Trent aimed its statement that original sin affects men and women 'by propagation and *not by imitation*' (DS 1513) against Pelagian views, which the Council of Carthage had first opposed in 418! The biological implications of Trent are clear. But by ruling out a particular doctrine of 'imitation' and ruling in 'propagation', Trent did not exclude other models for interpreting original sin and its transmission. Modern anthropology and sociology have raised possibilities never dreamt of, when a sixteenth-century council excluded a fifth-century piece of heterodoxy.

The historical contingencies which led to the defining of dogmas result in a third limitation. Dogmas have by no means equally interpreted all facets of Christian revelation. Belief about Christ's *person*, for instance, has received far more dogmatic attention than any beliefs about his *work*. We cannot expect dogmatic formulations to yield a comprehensive or even an intellectually satisfying account of God, Christ, man and the world. At many levels we find even the sum total of Christian dogmas to be 'ragged'. They lack finish and often offer little information in the face of urgent questions. How does salvation reach the non-evangelized? What are the criteria for an 'orthodox' interpretation of Christ's resurrection? How should we properly express the relationship of Church and Synagogue? What is the nature of the ordained ministry? From our standpoint even the complete history of defined dogmas frequently fails to answer important questions or get its emphases and proportions right. The particular challenges and needs which elicited dogmas have proved far too random to have produced any neat and comprehensive pattern even after two thousand years of Christianity.

A fourth and related limitation can be expressed by saying: All dogmas are equal but some dogmas are more equal than others.[4] Recently it has become fashionable to speak of a 'hierarchy of dogmas'. Many theologians used to differentiate dogmas necessary for salvation (*necessitas medii*) from those which were compulsory only if known (*necessitas praecepti*). They also contrasted (a) 'pure' dogmas, mysteries in the strict sense which can be known only through revelation, with (b) 'mixed' dogmas which may be known in varying degrees by natural reason. As such the notion of a hierarchy of dogmas focuses on their significance, rather than on man's cognitive access to them or their function as means to an end. The questions have ceased to be: How necessary for salvation is this or that dogma? Does man know this dogma through faith alone or partly through reason? When we now ask about degrees of significance, it is clear that some dogmas stand on a much higher level of importance than others. Chalcedon's formulations about Christ matter more than Trent's canons on the sacraments. Belief in Christ stands in judgement over any sacramental teaching, not vice versa. We can contrast central and peripheral truths. Central truths deal with Christ (or God) *in whom* we believe. Peripheral truths involve the Church, the sacraments and the Virgin Mary, in whom we may believe but only in a less fundamental sense than is the case with the central truths.

To prevent my argument from stepping off into dull obscurity let me introduce two sketches, labelled A and B :

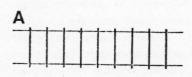

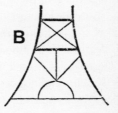

We should not imagine that dogmas have followed each other through history like roughly equal railway sleepers linked by rails of easy inference, as in A. We move closer to the truth if we use an image like an unfinished Eiffel Tower. In B the thicker lines represent more fundamental dogmatic formulations. Other statements make a criss-cross and still others look like curves. But all of these formulations lead us in one way or another towards God, even if they never reach and encapsulate his truth for all time.

That brings me to a fifth limitation on the value of dogmas, the *inadequacy* of human concepts and terms. Let me quote again *Mysterium Ecclesiae*, that 1973 declaration from the Sacred Congregation for the Doctrine of the Faith. It speaks of the 'mysteries of God' : 'Even if they are revealed to us and accepted by faith, they remain concealed by the veil of faith itself and are as it were wrapped in darkness' (art. 5). Dogmas deal with a mysterious and infinite Truth, the triune God revealed in Jesus Christ. Human thought and language remain always inadequate to describe this reality. The previous chapter in effect dealt with this point, when we discussed the central place of analogy in dogmatic formulations.

If the finite nature of human thought and language limits the value of dogmas, what follows? At least this. No definitions can reach a final point which would excuse future generations from reflecting further on the matter. No dogma can say to us : 'Set your mind (and your language) at rest about this truth.' Years ago Karl Rahner warned against any attempts to treat dogmas as such final, petrified conclusions : 'The clearest formulations, the most sanctified formulas, the classic condensations of the centuries-long work of the Church in prayer, reflection and struggle concerning God's mysteries all these derive their life from the fact that they are not end but beginning, not goals but means, truths which open the way to the ever greater Truth.'⁵ Some lines from T. S. Eliot's *Little Gidding* parallel curiously Rahner's reflection on the achievements of dogmatic language :

> . . . to make an end is to make a beginning.
> The end is where we start from.

Dogmas never take us anywhere. We arrive where we started from in our efforts to express the truth about the Father of Our Lord Jesus Christ. The mystery abides. Thomas Aquinas once observed that 'the revelation made to us in this life does not tell us what God is, and so our union with him is like union with an unknown Being'.

No dogma can tell us who or what God is. Even the most brilliant formulation cannot finally lift the veil of obscurity to allow us to say : 'Now I *know* God.'

Hence I feel very uncomfortable when Bernard Lonergan introduces method in science *and theology* as 'a normal pattern of recurrent and related operations yielding cumulative and progressive results'.[6] In Lonergan's view theology relies heavily on the dogmatic formulations which have piled up over the centuries. (With some critics I find that his theological method sits far too light both to the results of historical research and to biblical theology.) Can the theologian derive 'cumulative and progressive' results from the mass of past dogmas, so that he knows more about God than Augustine or Francis of Assisi because he has more dogmas to draw on? We can certainly enjoy such results in the field of science. We know more physics, chemistry and biology than Aquinas, Luther or Pascal. These sciences offer accumulated bodies of knowledge which can be enriched by progressive discoveries. In a sense theology accumulates information by drawing on the fresh findings of scriptural and historical studies —a phenomenon in which Lonergan hardly displays sufficient interest. But in its essential 'given' theology does not tolerate an increase, even through the most brilliant dogmatic definitions. Dogmas cannot turn theology into a progressive science. Foundational revelation closed with the apostolic age. The faith, Church proclamation and theology which responds to that revelation no longer experience 'any real increase from outside . . . The new justifies itself always and only through its origin from the old; the new truth is the old truth and not a truth added to the old one from outside.'[7] We can expect from dogmas and other features of the Church's life no more than what Eliot predicts in *Little Gidding* :

> We shall not cease from exploration
> And the end of all our exploring
> Will be to arrive where we started
> And know the place for the first time.

We can in no real sense hope for cumulative and progressive gains in our understanding and expression of the truth about God. Here believers and theologians resemble artists, writers and literary critics. No canons of criticism, no rules of painting and no norms of style can bring cumulative and progressive success in these fields, whether we focus on the community or individuals. Picasso's later works will not inevitably prove superior to his earlier works. Twentieth-century dramatists cannot stand on the shoulders of their predecessors from the sixteenth century A.D. or the fifth century B.C. to bring us a linear and undeniable advance in stage productions. No modern Leavis can offer us critical results which undeniably surpass those of Aristotle. In the realm of faith and theology, dogmas about Christ, the sacraments and the Church remain no more than diverse, analogous expressions which inadequately respond to the mystery of God. Our faith is endlessly engaged with the task of articulating itself. The wisest theologian or the holiest saint, even if supported by the full range of Church teaching and dogma, can hope for no more than to lose as gracefully as possible in his efforts to understand and speak of God. At the end Thomas Aquinas looked back at his work as so much straw, not as a mass of cumulative and progressive theological results.

OBJECTIONS TO DOGMA

So far in this chapter we have reviewed some major limitations on the value of dogmatic formulations. Never ultimate norms for faith, dogmas resulted from particular and contingent events in which believers struggled to express God's truth through inade-

quate human concepts. When compared with each other, dogmas look very uneven in their importance. In Chapter III we
suggested ways in which dogmatic formulations could function
in a healthy fashion to support Christian living. This account of
their limitations and functions enables us to return now to the
case against dogmas outlined in Chapter II and ask : How strong
is that case which we summarized under four words—liberty, reason, language and politics ?

First things first. Dogmas have often outrageously denied human and Christian *freedom*. There never was nor could be any
legitimate reason for torturing or executing one's brothers and
sisters for the sake of the gospel. Jesus offered an invitation :
'Come, follow me.' He asked : 'Will you also go away ?' He could
never have burnt anyone. St Paul acted like Jesus. On occasions
he took issue with Christian communities over developments
which tampered with central beliefs on justification and resurrection. Despite his anger at the Galatians for returning to justification by the works of the law, he argued, cajoled, criticized and
flattered them with only one aim in view—their free acceptance
of his conviction that salvation comes through faith in the crucified and resurrected Christ. Some Corinthian Christians had gone
astray in their attitude towards the resurrection. Paul never attempted to force their assent by commanding them to accept
orthodox doctrine. Rather he appealed to the general consensus,
scriptural testimony and a variety of arguments to persuade his
readers of their own accord to return to the truth (I Cor 15).

The violence done to man's conscience and liberty in the name
of dogmatic orthodoxy occurred because abstract principles sup-
planted the person of Jesus Christ. Human formulations of faith
became in effect the ultimate and absolute norm by which life or
death was sometimes decided. Our world needed to be made safe
from dogma. The history of persecutions carried on by Christians
was unspeakably bad. It is perfectly understandable that some
look back at that history and dismiss all dogmatic definitions as
pathological developments effected by Church authorities, who

no longer deserved to be called followers of Jesus Christ. Ideally any dogma invites us to praise God and commit ourselves to real faith in his Son. But many bishops, popes and inquisitors bypassed that invitation, ideologized Christianity and turned dogmas into norms of barren orthodoxy.

However, the desire for dogmas has frequently come 'from below' rather than 'from above'. Blame should be distributed fairly. All too often anthropological rather than theological or ecclesiological pressures lay behind the making and misuse of dogmas. Christian believers have required dogmatic formulations to fill a number of needs, even though that entailed restricting responsible freedom. First, they have looked to dogmas *to remove insecurity* above the nature and interpretation of their religious belief. They have found it threatening to live in proper Christian freedom without fixed and definite borders. Dogmas have helped them to order their experiences, as well as to interpret their biblical texts. Second, Christians want to be reassured about their *origins*. It is out of the question for most believers to investigate and recapitulate the birth and subsequent history of Christianity. Dogmas concerned with the institution of the Church, the creation of the sacraments and the privileges of the Virgin Mary summarize economically certain conclusions about Christian origins. These summaries lift a burden from the shoulders of many believers, and provide them with an access to the past which would otherwise remain closed to them. Dogmas resemble those social myths which reassure citizens about the early history of their country. A few classic formulations drawn from the Declaration of Independence and similar sources have offered many Americans a satisfying and sufficient account of how their country began.

Third, Christians have looked to dogmas to *identify* each other. To put this point negatively. Common dogmatic language served to identify and exclude any 'foreign devils', who refused to acknowledge Christ as 'one person in two natures', the Church as 'the one ark of salvation' or infant baptism as removing original sin. Lutherans spoke of 'scripture alone' and 'justification by faith alone'. Catholics talked of scripture *and* tradition, transubstantiation and the sacrifice of the Mass. Members of such linguistic communities forcibly demanded that others declare, 'I believe in original sin', 'I believe in papal infallibility' or 'I believe in justification by faith alone'—even if they admitted that, strictly speaking, one believed only in Jesus Christ himself. They forced their fellow-Christians to endorse fixed formulations because the pressure to identify 'our side' and 'the other side' overrode any scruple about curtailing freedom and doing violence to consciences. A community need lay behind this social pathology. Dogmas removed insecurity about mutual identification, but at the price of proper freedom. They have proved far more successful in identifying members of one's own group, than in mediating revelation and freeing people to find God. Three hundred years ago Glanvill castigated dogmas for supporting unions of sectarians:

> The union of a Sect within itself is . . . no concord of *Christians*, but a conspiracy against *Christ*; and they that love one another, for their *opinionative concurrences*, love for their *own sakes*, not their *Lords*: not because they have his *image*, but because they bear one *anothers*'.[8]

It remains, however, unfair to dismiss all dogmatic definitions as simply bad in themselves. The standard case has its point. At times of crisis Church leaders bore the responsibility to deal with confusion and respond to particular challenges. An old adage comments on past performance in this area: *Abusus non tollit usum* (abuse does not invalidate usage). Yet this adage needs also to be reversed: *Usus non tollit abusum*. Where dogmatic formulas did function healthily in Christian history, the memory of that appropriate usage does not allow us to brush off glibly the evil abuses committed in the name of orthodoxy.

Ultimately the question of principle proves more urgent than any balancing of historical uses and abuses. Are dogmatic formulations as such incompatible with human freedom? Can we regard dogmas as 'binding' on believers? Obligation involves two steps here. First, whether one finds Chalcedon, Lateran IV or Trent as particularly congenial or not, at those councils large and leading groups of our Christian predecessors chose to express their faith in solemn formulations. We owe them a *hearing*. Human faith in the God who disclosed himself through Jesus Christ comes about when one listens to the preaching of the Church (Rom 10 : 14–17). In the wider sense that preaching also includes the sacraments, teaching, the scriptures, sacred art, various styles of living and the proclamation of dogmas. Revelation reaches us because somehow we are addressed by our Christian contemporaries *or* predecessors. Different forms of community language can bring about revelatory situations, and initiate or renew the faith of adherents. Externally dogmas are 'binding' in the sense that they deserve to be heard. Right from the origins of the Jewish-Christian religion God has mediated his revelation through social and ecclesiastical channels. One significant channel has been the formulation of dogmas.

Second, our willingness to respond with understanding and sympathy *may* mean that a given dogma helps to generate for us a situation where God reveals himself. The Chalcedonian definition could deepen my appreciation of Christ's mysterious grandeur. Trent's canons on the sacraments may challenge my sinful disregard for full participation in sacramental life. Reading Pius IX's proclamation of Mary's immaculate conception might impress me with God's sovereign independence in calling us to salvation. Remembering these old dogmas may move beyond empty repetition to a lively re-enactment, in which the divine word reaches me in my new situation. Where a specific dogma renews an insight, communicates a message or evokes a religious feeling, it 'binds' me to follow that insight, accept that message or act on that religious feeling. In brief, dogmas oblige where they actually prove to be revealing. But there is no way of ensuring in advance that this will happen. Even *Mysterium Ecclesiae* recognizes as much. 'The dogmatic formulas', it insists, 'remain for ever suitable for communicating' revealed truth *'to those who interpret them correctly'* (art. 5; italics mine). How can anyone guarantee beforehand that this or that person, even with the best will in the world, is going to 'interpret them correctly'? Many causes can throttle the communication of revelation, not least the dead language in which old dogmas are cast.

Earlier I compared Church dogmas to a compost heap which had been piled up over the centuries. Antique furniture could provide a more helpful analogy. Late twentieth-century Catholics and other Christians are like people who have within their communities inherited houses that contain various pieces of antique furniture. They will, of course, examine attentively these pieces which their ancestors prized and bequeathed to them. The furniture may suit their own preferences and fit well into a tastefully arranged living room. Or, even though they respect their ancestors' tastes, they may prefer to store the pieces in an attic. The furniture remains an enduring part of the house and its history, but does not affect the daily life of the present generation. They are not *bound* to use the furniture in that way. We would in fact fear for their freedom and sanity, if through some misguided piety they held themselves obliged to fill the living room with the antiques, although they found them personally distasteful and unusable.

Finally, no one can claim for Church dogmas an equal, let alone a greater, binding force than Jesus or Paul claimed for their preaching. Neither Jesus nor Paul maintained : 'My formulations bind all of you to believe them now and forever. The only thing which can stop you doing so is your sinful refusal to believe.' Jesus preached, but only those 'drawn' by the Father could 'come' in faith to him (Jn 6 :44, 65). When through Paul's proclamation men reached 'the knowledge of the glory of God in the face of Christ', this was due to the God who once said, 'Let light shine out of darkness' and was now illuminating men's hearts to give them this knowledge by, as it were, a new act of creation

(II Cor 4:6). Man's acceptance of faith was a work of God to be compared with the original creation. Certainly men could wilfully refuse to accept Jesus' good news that God's power was breaking into our world, or Paul's message that God has raised the crucified Jesus from the dead. But human decision remains always subordinate to the divine initiative which calls men to belief when and where God wills. No dogma can be binding in the sense of automatically generating a situation of divine revelation. Such a claim would fly in the face of the clear New Testament message that God is free in disclosing himself. Paul offers the classic statement of this theme in chapters 9–11 of Romans. No other section of the scriptures stresses more the sovereign free election of God, who 'has mercy upon whomever he wills, and hardens the heart of whomever he wills' (9:18). Paul can only conclude with a cry of wonder before the mystery of God's electing call: 'How unsearchable are his judgements and how inscrutable his ways' (11:33). Excessive claims about the binding nature of dogmas can ignore this divine freedom as well as threaten human liberty.

In Chapter II I drew together a further set of arguments against Christian dogmas under the heading of *reason*. Here again one must confess with shame aberrations unworthy of the gospel. Rigid adherence to dogmas has led many believers to act irrationally, suppress the truth and show less than proper intellectual integrity. By immunizing themselves against criticism and correction, they often fell victim to illusion and deception, as well as proving dangerously intolerant to other men and women. Christian faith, even (or especially?) encouraged by a long history of dogmas, should never become what Peter Steele has described as 'a leap not only in the dark but as it were of the legless'. Neither dogmas nor preaching nor any other features of the Church's life give grounds for a latter-day voluntarism which represses critical questions. The choice does not lie between commitment to dogmatic Christianity and rational pursuit of truth, as if one could follow *either* faith *or* reason but not both.

Properly understood, dogmas seek to lead us to the disclosure of God in Christ. That is their only legitimate and ultimate purpose—to speak of Christ. If we question whether dogmatic formulations are essentially irrational, we must go further and ask whether the Christian faith itself is irrational. Jesus himself never invited his audience to renounce argument, ignore evidence and rely on the authority of divine revelation. His most characteristic form of teaching, the parables, aimed precisely to excite serious reflection. He consistently warned those who wanted to follow him to be open-eyed about the cost of discipleship (Matt 8:19–22; Mk 8:34ff.). John 20:29 ('Blessed are those who have not seen and yet believe') did not amount to saying: 'Blessed are they who have no grounds whatsoever for believing and yet believe.' The blessing looked to those future Christians who would lack the direct evidence which confronted Thomas but would, nevertheless, display the same commitment that his confession expressed. John's gospel hardly encourages us to disdain grounds for belief. Its obvious stress on the value of signs and the function of witnesses does not support a call to blind faith. Paul likewise never presented faith in Christ as a form of superstitious gullibility which involved intellectual suicide. In his second letter to the Corinthians, for instance, he reflects frankly on his own experiences as a wandering and suffering missionary. He concludes by inviting his readers to engage in a similar self-scrutiny: 'Examine yourselves, to see whether you are holding to your faith. Test yourselves' (13:5). Both Jesus and Paul represent faith as costly but not irrational.

The charge of irrationality against Christian dogmas and faith should not, however, be allowed to bully us into reviving some deistic version of religion within the bounds of reason alone. Faith is rational but not merely rational. Only a distorted view reduces faith to a simple prolongation of critical argument and historical knowledge. Even in the case of the most learned believer faith remains more than the conclusion of a carefully conducted examination of the evidence for Christianity. We go beyond the evidence to ask : How does the gospel message, mediated through preaching, the scriptures, dogmatic formulations and the other channels, make sense or fail to make sense within the context of our world? What questions of mine are answered by the revelation through Jesus Christ to which dogmas point? Do the Chalcedonian definition, the creeds and the rest of the testimony to Jesus Christ offered by the Church bring him alive for me? In what sense can he rescue me from my bewilderments and satisfy my needs? My personal experience does not excuse me from scrutinizing rationally the evidence for the claims made by creeds, dogmas and sermons. Rather it constitutes the context in which that evidence can be understood and appropriated.

To express my point another way. The acceptance of the Christian claims ties in with one's own hopes. If a man gives up hope, he gives up himself and simultaneously the possibility of personal assent to those claims. We cannot make such an assent without also answering what Camus identified as 'the only real philosophical question', that of suicide. Clearly, if less dramatically, Kant's third question at the end of his *Critique of Pure Reason* ('What may I hope for?') suggests that the truth or falsity of the central message which lies behind Christian dogmas will be decided only by reference to 'my' destiny. Belief in that message challenges me to revise my forecasts and forebodings of the future. This belief entails the conviction that my world is headed towards fulfilment, not mere ending or catastrophe.

Finally, as dogmas no less than any other elements of the Christian message call us to a relationship of loving faith in Jesus Christ, critical reason alone does not prove here either decisive or final. In the closing chapters of John's gospel it is the 'beloved' disciple who shows himself sensitively aware of his knowledge—a connection denied by the peculiarly modern prejudice that love is blind. According to that prejudice all true knowledge can come only through the careful control of our feelings, so that we can proceed with scientific objectivity to supposedly sound conclusions. Love, however, does recognize the truth, as Augustine, Goethe, Dostoevski and others have appreciated in their different ways. 'Give me a lover', cried Augustine, 'and he will understand.' The young Goethe wrote : 'We learn to know only what we love. The depth and fullness of our knowledge are proportionate to the strength, vigour and liveliness of our love and even our passion.' It was a reflection that Goethe would repeat and explore during a lifetime. In the closing pages of Dostoevski's *Crime and Punishment* love brings Raskolnikoff to acknowledge the reality of his existence. Under the impact of Sonia's devotion the hero finally glimpses the truth about himself and her. In a genuine sense only lovers have their eyes opened and can see the truth.

With respect to faith in Christ sheer reason and good sense alone fail to prove decisive. Nor are they final. One believes in the risen Christ without fully understanding his death and resurrection, the ways his Church has developed and, specifically, the values (and disvalues) of her dogmatic pronouncements. It is like believing in someone's love. You can say a lot, although you can say very little conclusively.

The heart has its reasons and love enables man to recognize reality. This can be forgotten by the champions of enlightened reason, scientific enquiry and intellectual integrity in their (partially justified) polemic against irrational adherence to dogmas. Joachim Kahl, for instance, leaves no middle ground between (1) a dogmatic reliance on authoritarian revelation which disdains rational verification, and (2) a 'pancritical rationality', which he describes as 'a way of thinking which is free of any external domination, always regards all assumptions and all results as in principle open to criticism and does not cling stubbornly and dogmatically to any thesis'.[9] Certainly those who capitulate to irrational dogmatism must learn to open themselves to criticism. Nevertheless, *sheer* rationality, pancritical or otherwise, does not adequately account for decisions which shape human lives—for instance, the passionate disillusionment with Christianity which moved Kahl to write his book. In the sphere of personal commitments rationality is necessary but insufficient. We cannot derive norms for life merely from scientifically established conclusions, mathematical axioms and the best results of critical reasoning. Our tastes, free choices, our emotions, experiences in personal relationships and many contingent events of our individual history offer grounds for fundamental decisions which reach far beyond the sphere of clear reason alone. The living reality of Christian dogmas, no less than of Christian faith itself, defies reduction simply to critical rationality.

The case against dogma has, of course, run in the opposite direction. Do dogmas represent anything more than a capitulation to rationalism, an abstract intellectualizing of the original concrete message and an unfortunate hellenization of Christianity? The standard response to this objection has dwelt on two themes. First, the official dogmas of the Church kept to limits in their involvement with philosophical terminology. Harnack, if he described dogma 'in its conception and its development' as 'a work of Greek spirit on the soil of the gospel', noted, nevertheless, that this hellenizing process took place 'on the soil of the gospel'.[10] Philosophy did not replace the New Testament message. Bernard Lonergan points out how the use of *homoousios* in the early Church councils 'does not determine what attributes are to be assigned to the Father and so must be assigned to the Son as well; it leaves the believer free to conceive the Father in scriptural, patristic, medieval, or modern terms'. Lonergan dwells on the ambiguity of other key terms (*persona, substantia, hypostasis* and *natura*) in maintaining that the Christology of the early Church 'offers an open structure', not a closed philosophical system.[11] In their most philosophical moods later councils declined to endorse solemnly and officially any system, even Aristotelianism. Trent stops perhaps short of that point. It did not expound the Eucharist as involving a substantial change (*mutatio substantialis*) through which the 'accidents' persisted. It spoke rather of substance and appearances (*species*) in describing what the 'wonderful conversion' (*mirabilis conversio*) entailed (DS 1652). But it should be admitted that the Tridentine decree on the Eucharist betrays a thoroughly Aristotelian frame of mind.

Second, we should not identify Church dogmas with all the speculations that have attached themselves to dogmas. Theologians have developed accounts of transubstantiation that sounded more like essays in supernatural physics than statements about what St Paul called 'announcing the death of the Lord until he comes'. Abstract language edged out concern with the living questions of Christian existence. It has taken more than Pascal and Kierkegaard to recall theologians from these aberrations. Finally, those who deny the charge that dogmas have fatally rationalized the gospel message will sometimes remind us of Vatican I's invitation to interpret the basic dogmas of Christian faith in the light of their relation to man's ultimate destiny (DS 3016). Dogmas aim to enlighten human existence, not to serve abstract speculation. Theologians, not Church councils, have been at fault.

It would be ungenerous not to appreciate the persuasive points made by those who in this way resist the Harnackian charges of rationalist corruption. However, they remind me of what one astronaut said of his colleague : 'He's all right, but a bit inclined to throw his weightlessness about.' The defence looks somewhat weightless, when it fails to take two points on board. First, even if the Christian religion has proved the greatest employment agency for philosophers the world has ever seen, the role of Greek philosophy in framing dogmas looks casual and contingent. If Christ had come in the late nineteenth century, theologians might well have used predominantly Weberian, Marxist, Durkheimian or Freudian categories in their work of elucidating the Christian gospel. In that case the influence of anthropological, economic, sociological and psychological concepts would have affected dogmatic formulations from the earliest Church councils. Whatever we say of the historical past, the danger of distorting the gospel message by alien rationalism goes beyond the use and abuse of philosophy.

That leads me to my second observation. Whether councils and popes used philosophical or other concepts to summarize and clarify Christian revelation, they had to move inevitably in the direction of abstraction. That procedure carried with it the danger of detaching believers from the concrete event of revelation. No one has warned us more clearly than G. C. Jung about the ways dogmas may replace immediate experiences and protect people against direct religious encounters. He wrote : 'A dogma is always the result and fruit of many minds and many centuries, purified of all the oddities, shortcomings, and flaws of individual experience. But for all that, the individual experience, by its very poverty, is immediate life, the warm red blood pulsating today.'[12] Dogmas speak of the events surrounding Christ's coming. They aim to liberate and guide men and women to a full life of faith. This makes it all the more intolerable when they become techniques for evasion. We outrageously misuse the Trinitarian dogmas of the early Church wherever we make them, in effect, serve as a defence mechanism against experiencing the Holy Spirit. Trent intended its Eucharistic dogmas to facilitate, not impede, the full impact of sharing in the sacrament. Usually dogmatic pronouncements directly or at least obliquely invoke the New Testament. We must take them at their word, if we wish to stop these dogmatic aids substituting (or being allowed to substitute) for the gospel message itself. Only constant confrontation with the New Testament will both ensure that dogmas do serve discipleship and help us to evade the dilemma : either dogmatic Christianity or the claims of Christ's love. The 'geography of dogma' can support us in our stand on the 'geography of faith'. The Chalcedonian Christ will never encourage anti-Semitism or other outrages for those who repeatedly recur to the first-century Galilean who invited us all : 'Come, follow me.'

The third set of objections against dogma which were outlined in Chapter II touch the sensitive area of *language*. Those objections will prove fatal unless we modestly qualify claims for dogmatic language. (1) This language cannot literally 'define' any aspect of God's saving activity towards mankind. At best it conveys glimpses and hints of the truth. It may succeed in evoking in us some appropriate reaction in the face of God's loving involvement with human history, but not through formulating with clear precision the truths of revelation. (2) In a situation of confusion pastoral reasons may make obligatory language advisable. But we must disavow any attempts to turn *homoousios*, transubstantiation or other terms into words of God. The need to safeguard unity, not some Sinaitic revelation, dictated conciliar choices here.

(3) Dogmatic language has on occasion replaced the full commitment of faith. Some Christians have misrepresented faith as if it were a bundle of isolated statements to be memorized or sworn to. Call this 'saying the right things' (orthology or orthophony). Let us not dignify such a barren subscription to words by the noble and traditional name of orthodoxy, or at least let us describe it as mere *verbal* orthodoxy. At best, this procedure reduces Christian theology to what could be called 'theologic', talk about talk about God. Theologicians content themselves with scrutinizing the geography of dogma, as they coordinate talk about God, interpret this religious language and draw conclusions from it. The classic account of theology as 'faith seeking understanding' applies only at second-hand. They seek to understand the faith-statements of others. Theologicians do not expound God, but formulations about God. At worst, their orthophony can conceal a betrayal of the Christian faith. The 'right' words remain, but the real meaning can misrepresent the gospel. Karl Rahner puts matters bluntly: 'It is quite possible for heresy to co-exist with verbal orthodoxy.'[13]

(4) Inspiration did not exempt the books of the bible from being conditioned by the changing states of human language and literature. Literary, form and redaction criticism has uncovered this historical quality of the biblical texts. We should avoid any

suggestion that by some miraculous superiority over the scriptures dogmas have enjoyed access to a supernatural, trans-historical language, which expressed revelation in timeless formulation. The 'deposit of faith' is not a bag of perennially true formulations which the Church guards and which make up the sum and essence of revelation. No council can distil out of the pure deposit of faith, which always appears in words and ideas conditioned by the changing language of a given period, as well as by the current culture and philosophy. Dogmas do not constitute a unique exception to the general mutability of human language. The dogmatic articulation of revelation, like the experience of revelation itself, is always provisional and changing. Just as the personal engagement of faith which responds to divine revelation must be renewed and grow, so faith's dogmatic statements need constant reformulation.[14] The use of a dead language (Latin) has created the linguistic illusion that it could raise dogmatic definitions above the usual limitations of space and time. But any language, even a dead language, can only be used by living men at a particular time of human history. Inevitable they will use Latin in ways shaped by the culture and thought-forms of the moment.

Key words in dogmatic definitions can and do change their meanings both in general usage and within the Church. Terms like 'faith', 'heresy' and 'error' enjoyed a wider range of meaning in the Middle Ages *and* at the Council of Trent than they did at Vatican I and later.[15] Nowadays 'person' suggests individual consciousness and freedom to the point that the classical Trinitarian formulations sound like expressions of belief in three Gods, Tritheism. Likewise 'substance' carries a contemporary meaning which is quite different from the scholastic concept found in the Middle Ages. Of course, such very simple confessions of faith as that 'God is three' or that 'Christ is present in the Eucharist' partially evade cultural and linguistic limitations. They transcend somewhat the normal contingencies of history. But, unlike most dogmas, they say very little. These two confessions leave open the kind of presence and trinity which faith acknowledges.

Admittedly re-formulation can conceal dishonest tampering. But where Christians refuse to re-conceptualize and re-formulate their dogmas, they will certainly both fail to communicate and risk distorting the truth. Their language becomes empty and unintelligible, because it has lost contact with the religious experiences it once dealt with. J. A. T. Robinson reflects on the fate of early dogmatic formulas concerning the Trinity :

> Originally the doctrine was created to describe, define and safeguard an experience. But in the process the experience seems to have drained right out of it, the dogma has become airborne, and we are asked if we believe in the formula as though this were what being a Christian means. We are left with a shell on our hands from which the life that shaped it has long since departed.[16]

Worse than this can occur. We grasp the meaning of any assertion in its context. Every context is subject to change. Hence maintaining what are verbally the same assertions in changed contexts entails shifts of meaning. Both Christian communities and the whole of mankind have experienced almost indefinitely many contexts of meaning. For instance, by repeating sixteenth-century formulations in the late twentieth century, we will not convey what the bishops at Trent might have meant—whatever else we do. 'Doctrines', Lonergan remarks, 'have meaning within contexts, and so, if the doctrines are to retain their meaning within the new contexts, they have to be recast.'[17] Loyalty to truth makes new formulations necessary. Even Vatican I required only that the original meaning of dogmas be preserved, not that the original set of words be endlessly repeated (DS 3020).

The bishops at Trent offer us an example in their teaching on the sacraments. They defined that Christ 'instituted' the seven sacraments of the New Covenant (DS 1601). What counted as sacramental 'institution' in their context differs from what might count as institution today. Modern biblical scholarship, along with many other historical changes, has shifted the context in which we hear assertions about the origin of the sacraments. Unlike our sixteenth-century predecessors, we cannot, for instance, presume that the Great Commission at the end of Matthew ('Go therefore and make disciples of all nations baptizing them', etc.) was actually spoken by the risen Christ. If an evangelist saw baptismal implications in the resurrection and put his interpretation on the lips of the risen Christ, would that suffice to speak of baptism as 'instituted' by Christ? Or is the institution of all the subsequent sacraments of the Church adequately authorized by the historical Jesus' actions in calling men and women to form around him a community of disciples? These questions shape our context, but they do not reach back to the time of the reformation and Trent.

Lastly, only a false purism would deny that Christian dogmas make oblique statements about the political and social order. That much should be conceded to the fourth set of objections, which cluster under the heading of *politics*. We need to unmask the political causes and implications of dogmas. However, to admit that right from the Council of Nicaea dogmas have a political face does not amount to reducing them *merely* to oblique statements about the state of society. The complex interrelation that one can normally detect between the political order and the proclamation of dogmas illustrates well how sacred and secular elements can intertwine in human affairs. In two ways dogmatic definitions have carried implications for secular politics. There were the direct connections—for instance, between Christological dogmas and civil authority in the Roman Empire. The emperors convoked early Church councils and derived support for their own position from the progressive proclamation of the divine person and nature of Christ. As councils acclaimed more and more clearly the kingly majesty of the heavenly Christ, this process helped to justify the earthly rule of Roman monarchs.

Second, dogmas usually *look back* to the origins of Christianity or even earlier. Original sin occurred at the birth of the human race, Christ instituted seven sacraments, he endowed his Church with infallibility and so forth. This orientation towards the past has a stabilizing function. Its concern with origins serves the cause of social consolidation.

It has become conventional to note the *conservative* political force of dogmas. What can be overlooked is their role as a form of *liberating protest*. What I have in mind goes beyond such future-oriented dogmatic formulations as those concerned with the coming resurrection of the dead. Obviously these beliefs protest that sin and death do not enjoy the final victory. I think rather of the emancipating implications of Chalcedon's Christological confession or Pius IX's definition of Mary's immaculate conception. Chalcedon recognized that Christ was 'of one substance with us as regards his manhood'. This confession radically protested against the system of slavery, which in effect denied that Christ shared a human nature with *all* of us. But Christians as a group failed for well over a thousand years to realize the liberating impact of their official Christology. Likewise, the proclamation of the immaculate conception acknowledged that a woman ranked as the most perfectly redeemed human person. This dogma challenged male attitudes both inside and outside the Church, which have long denied equal treatment to the other sex. It was a liberating protest against the inferior status of women, even it it was not seen to be so at the time. The usual accounts speak of dogmas as 'binding on all the faithful'. Chalcedon and Pius IX's bull *Ineffabilis Deus*, in fact, 'bound' Christians to free *all* their brothers and sisters for a life of equal dignity and responsibility.

To conclude. The call to unmask the political causes and implications of Christian activity usually looks beyond dogmatic formulations. Not only dogma but the full range of Church life has been rejected as the opium of the people, the means whereby the ruling capitalists keep the proletariat in a state of resigned submission. Elsewhere I have attempted to respond to this challenge from Karl Marx and others.[18] Whatever judgements one passes on that broader debate, writers of the enlightenment like Holbach have been shown to be naïve. Christian dogmas were no simple 'error', which blocked the enjoyment of freedom and which men could remove with the help of critical analysis. Natural happiness did not automatically follow the rational rejection of those dogmas. The enlightenment failed to produce consistent virtue. Rational progress has helped to open the way for new dogmas and ideologies which have meant death and enslavement for millions. The rise of modern technology has brought vast exploitation. Millions lived, and live, in insanitary poverty to spend their lives toiling in hideous factories, those 'dark, satanic mills'. Progress through scientific reason could make possible what has happened in Auschwitz, Dresden, Hiroshima and Vietnam. Somehow the eighteenth-century campaign against dogmatic error has failed to free the human race for a state of unruffled natural happiness.

V

Boundaries and Meaning

The mind understands only what it has created.
W. Dilthey, *Der Aufbau der Geschichtlichen
Welt in den Geisteswissenschaften*

The dogma of the Assumption . . . I consider to be the
most important religious event since the Reformation.
C. G. Jung, *Psychology and Religion*

WE HAVE BEEN disentangling, limiting and defending the functions of those Church pronouncements commonly classified as
dogmas. The discussion was primarily intended to elucidate the
ways in which such pronouncements have served (and could
serve) as guides and incentives to Christian living. The account
offered may also have helped to reduce the impetus of standard
arguments against dogmas.

But it is time to turn from generalities to particulars, from
discussing dogmas in general to ask: What constitutes a given
dogma? What is the *unity* with which we must deal? Secondly,
how should we clarify and establish the *meaning* of that unity?

THE UNITY OF DOGMA

Our first question has frequently drawn a minimalizing, quasi-
legal answer. Only the central words of definition constitute a
given dogma. In the case of Mary's assumption: 'We pronounce,
declare and define it to be a dogma divinely revealed: That the

immaculate Mother of God, Mary ever-virgin, her earthly life ended, was assumed body and soul into the glory of heaven' (DS 3903). Such a minimalizing approach might even maintain that a single word, *theotokos* (Mother of God), formed the dogma at the Council of Ephesus in A.D. 432 (DS 251, 252). The adoption of this one term would form the essential point to be examined and elucidated. Such a concentration on some central sentence or even some central word reminds me of attempts to reduce the unity of the Mass to the consecration. At their worst, these attempts were aimed at clarifying a mere handful of words from the Last Supper and the repetition of that text.

By fastening on to the key words and central statements of dogmas, Cardinal Franzelin and other minimalizers wanted to delimit the domain of valid and authoritative meaning. They aimed to counteract the exaggerations of ultramontanes like W. G. Ward, who ran wild in crediting a wide range of papal and conciliar pronouncements with dogmatic value. 'This and no more', argued the minimalizers, formed the binding definition which the faithful were to accept. Selections of dogmas, creeds and other official documents like Bettenson and Denzinger both enshrine and encourage the reductionist attitude. Thus the latest editor of Denzinger's *Enchiridion Symbolorum*, Adolf Schön-metzer, introduced his extract from the bull *Unam Sanctam* (November 18, 1302) with the comment: 'The final sentence alone is a dogmatic definition (*unice sententia finalis est definitio dogmatica*).'

It looks thoroughly artificial to follow the reductionist line and pick out a narrow set of 'operative words', while passing over other items in a given pronouncement. When delivering themselves of dogmas, council fathers and popes presumably intended to communicate through all that they said (and did). We would need good evidence to decide otherwise. What the reductionists encouraged was the quest for a clear, extrinsic norm of faith. As they understood divine revelation to consist in the communication of truths about God which would otherwise have remained inaccessible to man, they looked to a set of brief dogmatic formulas to provide secure access to this revelation. A relatively few defined propositions contained the essence of revelation. Against these guidelines faith could be clearly tested. This concentration on key sentences resembled the parallel quest for proof texts in scripture. One clear statement in St Paul was thought to resolve matters about the Eucharist, the Church, the divinity of Christ or whatever else was being debated. It has long since been recognized that we will misrepresent Paul, for instance, unless we reflect on the entire letter in question, or even on all his letters within the context of various New Testament theologies. If we cannot continue to treat the scripture with the old fishing-rod method, plucking 'operative' sentences from papal bulls or conciliar definitions should also be ruled out.

Another way of dealing with our issue is to look for *the* question to which some given dogmatic pronouncement sought to respond. In that case the unity on which we should concentrate would turn out to be a central question, not some key statement as such. George Vass encourages this approach when he writes: 'I regard Christian truth as an interpretation whose truth-value is primarily to be found in the questions it asks and secondarily in the answers it gives.'[1] Our search for the unity in Pius XII's definition of the assumption should lead us then to establish either (1) a more general question, or (2) a more specific question to which the pope intended to reply. Examples of (1) might be: Is there life after death? Is motherhood open to the highest honours? Instances of (2) might be: Where is Mary today? Has the Church's celebration of the feast of her assumption been soundly based? We could handle Boniface VIII's bull *Unam Sanctam* in similar fashion. There we read: 'We declare, announce, define and proclaim that subjection to the Roman Pontiff is absolutely necessary for salvation, for every human being' (DS 875). Does the truth-value lie primarily in some general, not specifically Christian question: Must a human

being pay allegiance to a religious leader if he wishes to be saved?
Or in some overtly Christian question: Does God absolutely require subjection to the bishop of Rome?

Nicholas Lash briefly raises the key objection against this way
of settling the essential point of the assumption or any other
dogma. 'Whether philosophers', he writes, 'will be happy with
the concept of truth-values attaching to *questions*, remains to be
seen.'[2] Questions can be 'right', 'correct' and 'helpful'. But there
are no 'informative' questions. As such they lack the capacity to
inform or describe. They have no referential aspect and hence
no truth aspect. To ask a question does not result in saying anything true or false. Further, the Council fathers at Chalcedon, Pius
XII and other Christian leaders who have contributed to our dogmatic inheritance clearly intended to make informative
statements. It would have been news to Pius XII in 1950 or
Boniface VIII in 1302 that their primary intention was to put a
question! Finally, we need to decide which question Pius XII
raised. Was it a general, not specifically Christian, question
about the right acknowledgement of motherhood? Or was it a
particular (Christian) question about Mary's state today? To
reach a reasonable solution we could only turn to the pope's
positive statements and other historical *information.* In other
words, we would move beyond the level of right or wrong questions to offer our own answer as to what was uppermost in Pius'
thoughts. We require information to know that we are truly asking the same questions as the pope.

To sum up. Any adequate investigation of dogmatic utterances
from Chalcedon, Trent or Pius XII must involve a scrutiny of
the questions being raised and the problems being faced. Nevertheless, a given dogma is not constituted by a correct (or in-
correct) question. We face another kind of unity when we ask:
What was the dogma of Mary's assumption? We deal primarily
with the meaning of statements, not the correctness of questions.
Answers and information inevitably assert their primacy here
over sheer questions.

A third way of deciding exactly what a particular dogma is might be to link it with a large slice of (earlier and later) religious language and activity. Any dogmatic statement enjoys borders peopled by other statements. Can we afford to dissociate 'this' dogma from the prior statements, debates, practices and institutions which led up to it? Dare we exclude the reception it met with, the problems it left unsolved and its final status from the given unity whose meaning we wish to clarify? Do all the causes, connections and consequences belong to a specific dogma? How can we, for instance, fix the boundaries for a history of the dogma of the immaculate conception? If we may not pass judgements until we have heard the whole story, how far does the whole story extend? Up to 1854? To 1870? To 1950 and beyond? Almost inevitably those theologians who study the development of dogma take a larger rather than a smaller focus. The unity with which they concern themselves is the continuity between dogmatic affirmations rather than the individual affirmations as such.

Beyond question, to understand the words which some given dogma uses we must recall the chain of usage which those religious expressions have already experienced (and much else besides). We dare not ignore the (frequently complicated) religious, sociological, psychological and political processes which brought these words to the lips of council fathers or popes. Nevertheless, *this* dogma, statement of faith, conciliar pronouncement, or however we finally decide to classify it, remains uniquely itself. Little is to be gained by denying that *this* is the unity which we must face, and in the name of doctrinal development dissolving it into some Heraclitean stream in which its boundaries disappear forever.

THE MEANING OF DOGMA

What then was being said in what was said? What did (and does) the Christological confession of Chalcedon, the bull *Unam Sanctam*, the definition of papal infallibility at Vatican I and

Pius XII's proclamation of the Assumption *mean*?

Three lines of approach can be discarded quickly: the covert introduction of (1) causes, (2) intended purposes or (3) *de facto* effects. To announce, for instance, that Vatican I's definition 'meant' the triumph of infallibilists does nothing more than point to impulses which gave rise to the dogma. The effort to trace the interlocking political, social and religious causes that produced some authoritative statement may be interesting and important. But as such the causality line fails to pin down the meaning of the statement in itself. We must revert to the question: What did the bishops at Vatican I intend to convey by their pronouncement of papal infallibility? What did they wish to communicate by their utterance, or rather endorsement, of certain sentences?

We likewise evade the central issue if we remain content to point to aims, objectives and purposes. We might satisfy ourselves that Pius XII proclaimed Mary's assumption because he *meant* to encourage 'many restless and anguished souls', those who could 'no longer believe in the goodness of life'.[3] If he wanted the definition to renew holiness among Catholics, did he hope that through divine providence this would help to secure a quicker victory over the anti-God forces of Communism? Admittedly, the pope could have indulged strong hopes for such consequences. Yet why did he pick *this* method for achieving his purposes and *this* doctrine for solemn definition? He could conceivably have defined solemnly related doctrines like (1) Christ's resurrection as such, or (2) the saving power of the crucifixion and resurrection. What did he find particularly appropriate about belief in Mary's assumption? What did he understand and wish to convey by his utterance about this belief? Three things need to be said. He intended (1) to bring his audience to think that he strongly believed something (namely, that as a total human person Mary enjoys heavenly glory), (2) to activate or re-activate this belief in his audience, and (3) to bring about as a natural consequence certain describable results (for instance, greater holiness through increased devotion to Mary). Some conscious objective as such did not constitute the proper *meaning* of his statement. It is playing with words to gloss over points (1) and (2) and allege that (3) formed 'the meaning' of the pope's pronouncement.[4] Motivation must not be confused with meaning.

If the meaning of a Christian dogma consisted in some aim, we should have to sort out proximate from ultimate aims, as well as—what would largely amount to the same thing—general religious aims from specifically Christian aims. The proximate aim of Pius' definition was presumably honouring the Virgin Mary in the Holy Year of 1950. 'Helping people to salvation' would rate as an ultimate objective. 'Serving God as faithfully as possible' could stand as the general religious aim, while we might consider 'giving final dogmatic authority' to an ancient doctrine the specifically Christian purpose of the pope's action. If we identify meaning and purpose, we would ultimately have to resolve even such a dogma as Mary's assumption into a broad religious aim about salvation and obedience to God. That would detect as 'the' meaning of this dogma something not even specifically Christian, let alone Catholic.

Thirdly, we might maintain that the proclamation of the assumption as an official dogma 'meant' support for the capitalist countries in their opposition to communism both in Europe and in Asia. The Korean war had been raging for some months prior to the pope's solemn act of definition. E. G. Selwyn, the Dean of Winchester, reacted against two articles in the *Civiltà Cattolica* which seemed to take such a line. He suggested that this would make 'the Madonna little more than a Boadicea of the United Nations'.[5] It looks historically true to assert that what happened in the Vatican on November 1, 1950, gave support to American policies in Europe and Asia. But I cannot draw from this historical judgement the conclusion that the pope meant just that by his definition. His utterances may well have entailed or effected such support. But it is as false to reduce *his* meaning to such *de facto* effects, as it is to identify his meaning with consciously intended purposes.

That brings us to the method believers instinctively adopt for clarifying the meaning of some dogma, *paraphrasing*. At worst, this amounts to using council fathers or popes as the mouthpiece for our own convictions. In a sense unintended by him we can exemplify Antoine de St Exupéry's dictum : 'Truth is not what we discover but what we create.' At best, paraphrasing offers a way of both respecting the original meaning and allowing for shifts of meaning which represent the state of individual believers and communities in their personal struggles for enlightenment. D. H. Lawrence's aphorism will have to be changed : Never trust the speaker, trust your own paraphrases. All of this needs to be elucidated at length.

Let me insist at the outset that personal paraphrasing should not permit us to misrepresent what the original statement meant —at least in the case of a pope. (As we shall shortly argue, we cannot speak of 'the' primary meaning of conciliar dogmas, which in fact constitute the overwhelming majority of dogmas.) Even when (as often happens) a pope fails to formulate explicitly his intentions, nevertheless, the context, general usage and public conventions governing the recognition of words normally indicate what he wished to convey. We suffer no special handicap from the fact that dogmatic definitions from popes never offer an infallibly guaranteed account of their meaning. (If such an account were added, we would require a further infallibly guaranteed account of the account, and so on *ad infinitum*!) P. F. Strawson is reassuring : 'We may expect a certain regularity of relationship between what people intend to communicate by uttering certain sentences and what those sentences conventionally mean.'[6] We would usually require good evidence before agreeing that some papal sentences expressed a hidden meaning which differed from their conventional sense. A strong prior disposition on our side to find a favourable or an unfavourable meaning hardly excuses us from dispensing with such evidence, when we wish to allege such a hidden meaning.

For these reasons I would part ways with Nicholas Lash over his interpretation of Boniface VIII's bull *Unam Sanctam*. In the name of the 'historical context' he argues :

> The problem to which the pope is addressing himself is not any theoretical theorem in soteriology or even ecclesiology, but a conflict concerning the respective socio-political authority of the pope and the king of France. Boniface VIII wished to assert the transcendence of God's kingdom—in relation to which all human community is provisional and subordinate. The theologian therefore recasts the papal definition in terms which take these considerations into account and, accordingly, is able to assess it as meaningful and true . . . We should not take it for granted, even in apparently quite straightforward cases, that we know what a given statement from our doctrinal past *meant*.

Lash's recast papal definition would run : 'We declare, announce, define and proclaim that all human community is provisional and subordinate to God's transcendent kingdom.'[7] This blunts the aggressive 'Roman' punch. But does it in fact convey the same information as the original statement? A conflict 'concerning the respective socio-political authority of the pope and the king of France' formed the context for Boniface's definition. The pope *could* have reflected on that conflict in the terms suggested by Lash. Appropriate words were available. However, Boniface chose different words : 'We declare, announce, define and proclaim that subjection to the Roman Pontiff is absolutely necessary for salvation, for every human being.' General usage and the social conventions governing the recognition of his meaning lead us to conclude that he meant just what those words said : Subjection to the bishop of Rome is absolutely necessary for anyone to be saved. It is highly doubtful that the proposed recasting of the definition represents what this 'given statement from our doctrinal past *meant*'. The recast definition amounts to a contemporary paraphrase, the reflections in faith evoked now by the words of a medieval pope. This is what the statement means *now* to Lash, not what it meant *then* on the lips of Boniface VIII.

Let us take another example where paraphrases might easily misrepresent the original meaning. Conceivably we could interpret Pius XII's definition of Mary's assumption as offering a radical political critique of the post-World War II situation. In effect we would not be locating this critique among the causes, intended purpose or *de facto* consequences of the definition, but arguing that this is what emerges if we unmask precisely what the pope meant. Was it then the essential meaning and point of his pronouncement that God would triumph over atheistic materialism, or even that Mary would be the hidden but real leader in some military victory over Communist countries? Once again preoccupation with the historical context, in this case the closing years of Stalin's reign, might lead us astray. Obviously Pius XII was deeply concerned about the persecution of Catholics in Eastern Europe, the victory of Mao Tse-tung in China and the growing strength of global Marxism. But did he say one thing ('Mary was assumed into heavenly glory') and mean another ('God will triumph over Communism')? He had at his disposal an adequate vocabulary to prophesy defeat for Marxist regimes. Normal usage and rules governing the recognition of meaning strongly suggest that Pius XII meant precisely what he said. Paraphrases which picture the Virgin Mary as a heavenly Boadicea at the head of the United Nations forces misinterpret *his* meaning.

It becomes, however, difficult, if not downright implausible, to speak of 'the original meaning' of dogmas when we turn to conciliar pronouncements. Suppose we managed to buttonhole several bishops as they left the Council of Chalcedon, the Council of Trent or Vatican I, and questioned them about documents to which they had just given their approval. Let us imagine we interrogated some Tridentine bishops about certain sections of their 1547 decree on the justification of the unrighteous, or several Chalcedonian bishops about their definition of Christ's 'two natures'. They would all offer some paraphrase but they would not say the same thing. Identical items in the conciliar documents would evoke from them differing paraphrases, reactions and interpretations. We would have to speak of the minds of the bishops rather than the mind of a council. The one conciliar statement could convey many meanings. The aftermath of Chalcedon clearly showed how Church leaders differed in their interpretations of the conciliar definition. The fact that the Moslems soon overran the 'Monophysites' has tended to obscure the seriousness of these differences. Any attempts to represent Chalcedon as clearly conveying the unified Christological understanding of an undivided Church fly in the face of historical evidence.

Conciliar definitions arose normally as compromise statements after long debates and were frequently left ambiguous to allow for a wide range of meaning. In defining papal infallibility at Vatican I some bishops clearly attached the strongest possible sense to the affirmation that 'the definitions of the Roman Pontiff are irreformable of themselves and not by virtue of the consent of the Church (*Romani Pontificis definitiones ex sese, non autem ex consensu Ecclesiae, irreformabiles*)' (DS 3074). Other bishops understood these words in the weakest possible sense. Given that conciliar dogmas are the products of committees, it looks dubious to speak confidently of one original meaning. A radical ambiguity discourages us from offering a simple, non-valent answer on either side. We may not read the most rigorous meaning into the words, nor may we try reductionism and give them the weakest possible sense. From the outset conciliar dogmas display an ineradicable ambiguity and plurality of meaning. Some alleged 'original meaning' simply cannot be caught in a net of words. As regards Church councils, therefore, I want to register sharp dissent from the view endorsed by Lonergan (a) that there once was a single meaning, and (b) that we can ascertain it. He writes: 'What permanently is true, is the meaning of the dogma in the context in which it was defined. To ascertain that meaning there have to be deployed the resources of research, interpretation, history, dialectic.'[8]

Undoubtedly some readers are asking themselves: Does O'Collins flatly deny the Vatican I instruction (DS 3020) that 'when once holy mother Church has declared the meaning of sacred dogmas that meaning must be forever retained (*sacrorum dogmatum is sensus perpetuo est retinendus, quem semel declaravit sancta mater Ecclesia*)'? Surely this statement implies *one* original meaning? 'Holy mother Church' includes the popes. In the case of papal definitions we can speak of 'the meaning' of a given pope proclaiming some new dogma. (If legal minimalism is the game, that satisfies the demands of Vatican I!) Conciliar definitions, however, differ, as I have argued. Even when they were first solemnly promulgated, these definitions conveyed various meanings. Moreover, councils normally 'declared' dogmas; they did not declare what those dogmas meant. Their audience had to gather the meanings of these formulations for themselves. It is out of the question to expect complete rational clarification and total certitude in this matter. Even if councils 'declared' the meaning of dogmas, they would need to set out also the meaning of the meaning, and so on *ad infinitum.*

How can we clarify the relationship between the official dogmas of councils or popes and subsequent paraphrases? It is antiquarian to confine our investigation of meaning to examining what a given dogma might originally have meant—for instance, the proclamation of Mary's assumption on the lips of Pius XII. Failure to acknowledge what this dogma meant to others would be a King Canute-like posture which refused to accept the rising tide of history. The paraphrases begin quickly.

A gap grew between the pope's apparent meaning and the subsequent interpretations of his pronouncement. Two paraphrases which appeared within days of Pius XII's solemn definition came from François Mauriac and C. C. Martindale. Where the French novelist spoke of 'the dogma' and 'the flesh' and the English Jesuit referred to 'the doctrine' and 'the realm of matter itself', in both cases the pope's action evoked primarily their belief in resurrection as such. Mauriac wrote : 'But we Christians do we really believe in eternal life? The dogma of the Assumption . . . draws our attention to that article of the Creed, the most mysterious, the most incredible, which is so rarely discussed by the Church and which represents an insane, a marvellous hope—the resurrection of the flesh.'[9] Martindale's letter to *The Times* suggested : 'If the doctrine of the Assumption be deeply studied, it will be seen to reproclaim the supremacy of spirit, and its triumph not only in spite of material forces, but within the realm of matter itself.'[10]

Two years later C. G. Jung offered a paraphrase and interpretation of the dogma of Mary's assumption in his *Answer to Job*. While recognizing how the pope's declaration was 'a slap in the face for the historical and rationalistic view of the world', he saw 'more in it than papal arbitrariness', and argued that 'the meaning not only of the new dogma but of all more or less dogmatic assertions' must be found 'over and above their literal concretism.'[11] Those who remained content to describe and analyse the formal meaning of dogmas could allow the real history to slip through their fingers. Jung made three claims about Pius XII's definition. In 'the truly apocalyptic world situation today' the papal declaration gave 'comforting expression' to 'that yearning for peace which stirs deep down in the soul', that 'expectation of divine intervention' arising 'in the collective unconscious and at the same time in the masses'. Secondly, if 'the signs of the times . . . point to the equality of women', this 'equality requires to be metaphysically anchored in the figure of a "divine" woman', the personal representation of 'the feminine'.

Thirdly, while the dogma of the assumption does not 'mean that Mary has attained the status of a goddess', nevertheless, her position as 'mistress of heaven' satisfies 'the need of the archetype', the feminine in God.[12] For 'it was recognized even in prehistoric times that the primordial divine being is both male and female'.[13] In Pius' definition of the assumption Jung found all this voiced: the longing for peace, a metaphysical anchor for the equality of women and a recognition of the feminine in God.

These three samples from a novelist, a popularizing theologian and a psychologist can serve to illustrate how paraphrases move away from the original meaning of a dogma. There is much linguistic continuity. Mauriac, Martindale and Jung all pin their remarks onto Mary's assumption. But the pope's definition has drawn from them such statements that their meaning or rather meanings at best remain only within hailing distance of his. We are faced not with a gap of centuries like the distance between Boniface VIII in 1302 and Nicholas Lash in 1973. Within a very few days or years paraphrases appear in which the sentiments expressed reveal a family resemblance—perhaps even a strong resemblance—to Pius XII's original utterance, but no exact identity of meaning. This was the case too with Karl Rahner's celebrated piece of 1951. 'The interpretation of the Dogma of the Assumption'. He proposed to discuss 'the inner meaning' or 'what is actually meant by the new dogma of Mary's bodily assumption into final perfection'.[14] His own theology took Rahner's exposition some distance from the pope's meaning.

Must we then choose between (1) the pope's original meaning and (2) the meanings of subsequent paraphrases? If we insist on the authoritative claims of (1) and expect Roman Catholics to remain exactly faithful to Pius XII's meaning, we appear to revert to that rigidly formal and merely extrinsic adherence to dogmas which has disfigured the Church's history. Yet plumping for (2) looks like a decision to let the claims of Church authority, even in its most solemn teaching, go to the wall.

H.D.A.F.—D

Ultimately we break the dilemma by recognizing that in fact we have our own personal paraphrases which, ideally, we reach in the light of both (1) and (2). We find reliable bearings here only by maintaining : Never simply trust any of the speakers, trust your own paraphrases. As with Jung, Rahner and the rest, Pius XII's words will evoke differing reactions from us. We bring to his statement our own questions, our own experiences and the insights which cluster about the religious language that is familiar to us. No pope, theologian or psychologist can dictate the questions which spontaneously arise for each of us, the deeper experiences that weave the web of our inner lives, the insights which certain religious analogies provoke, or the precise scope of the language which actually opens up God's revelation for us. Andres Tornos remarks that 'we can speak of a chain of momentary uses of religious expressions in the constant social event of human communication. *This claim takes words out of our control.*'[15] We need to go beyond that position. It is not simply the case that Church councils and popes can finally dictate neither the earlier nor later history of the language they adopt. It lies beyond their control to regulate the insights actually reached in the light of their statements. These insights will in their turn generate personal paraphrases, in which the meaning conveyed will not necessarily be four-square with the meaning(s) of the conciliar or papal statements that provoked them. This will all the more readily occur where the dogma in question is more complex. Thus any personal paraphrase of Mary's immaculate conception will depend upon one's understanding of original sin, redemption and divine foreknowledge.

At times Church authorities have tried to inhibit personal paraphrases, enforce fixed terminology and through moral or, worse, physical coercion enforce an assent to certain verbal formulations. In such cases sheer usage and ordinary conventions governing the recognition of meaning might prove less reliable than is usually the case. Speakers might keep the agreed words but in fact change, consciously or unconsciously, the meaning.

Here usage of an artificially standard kind could conceal altered meaning.

Let me add some further considerations in support of the principle, 'Never simply trust the speaker, trust your own paraphrases.' Firstly, neither councils nor popes ever say everything. In relation to what might have been said, relatively few things are said. The reality of any situation always extends beyond what people actually say at the time. This point goes beyond the familiar observation that dogmas more often than not have been aimed at excluding errors. They have frequently been clearer about what they rule out than what they rule in. Nevertheless, even where the positive elements predominate over the negative exclusion or errors, *dogmas say relatively few things.* Personal paraphrases take matters further. The elaboration does more than simply *add* new statements and meanings alongside the original statement and meaning. Qualitative shifts occur. The continuing paraphrases express fresh insights of believers in their historical struggle for enlightenment.

Secondly, the things said in religious discourse—as is the case with poetry—can say much more than the speaker intended or realized. He can have spoken more truly than he intended, or even have spoken truly in spite of himself. A gap can easily grow between what was meant and what was said. Michel Foucault develops this theme persuasively :

We know—and this has probably been the case ever since men began to speak—that one thing is often said in place of another; that one sentence may have two meanings at once; that an obvious meaning, understood without difficulty by everyone, may conceal a second esoteric or prophetic meaning that a more subtle deciphering, or perhaps only the erosion of time, will finally reveal; that beneath a visible formulation, there may remain another that controls it, disturbs it, and imposes on it an articulation of its own; in short that in one way or another, things sair say more than themselves.[16]

We might apply this point with outrageous exaggeration and say : Many a true word has been spoken in dogma.

Thirdly, what the passage of time reveals is that conciliar or papal dogmas, once announced, may later disclose a special point for movements which either do not yet exist or at best are so far scarcely visible. Let me take a contemporary example. Beneath the manifest political and economic history of the modern world we can glimpse by now that some serious, perhaps truly fundamental, but hitherto largely concealed developments have been at work. One of these has been the liberation of women. It could well be that, when all the evidence is in, the definitions of the immaculate conception in 1854 and the assumption in 1950 will be seen to have given timely religious expression to Mary as personal representative of the feminine principle. Beyond their intentions, Pius IX and Pius XII recognized in Mary the liberated woman and the needed counter-weight to a male-oriented, patriarchal religion. Admittedly, both Rome (through the two Vatican Councils) and the World Council of Churches responded to and encouraged developments in ecclesiological thinking and concerns. The Church can be pictured as mother of the faithful and bride of Christ. Yet such maternal and bridal images remain abstract and allegorical when contrasted with the Marian definitions, which anchor the female principle of religion in a concrete person.

This chapter began with the attempt to clarify the issue of dogmatic meaning. It became clear that it is misleading to speak of 'the' meaning of a given dogma. From the outset there may exist a plurality of meaning, as is the case with conciliar definitions. Even if we start from a papal definition where, presumably, one meaning is intended, personal paraphrases both inevitably and rightly introduce shifts of meaning. If it proves misleading to talk of 'the' meaning of dogmas, what of the term 'dogma' itself? Perhaps we should after having used it so far in this work, finally decided to answer the question expressed in the title by saying : 'No. Dogma should not have a future. But conciliar expressions of faith, creeds, papal pronouncements and other more or less solemn statements of faith have a future.' Is some challenge to 'dogma' as a commonly accepted classification called for?

VI
The End of 'Dogma'?

That the past is different from the present is a hard
doctrine.

A. J. P. Taylor, 'Fiction in History'

It is a frequent habit, when we discover several re-
semblances between two things, to attribute to both
equally, even on points in which they are in reality
different, that which we have recognized to be true of
only one of them.

René Descartes, *Regulae*

UP TO THIS point we have made use of 'dogma' as a classification. Readers who may have disagreed with my views will at
least have shared the classification with me. This sharing has
also characterized the recent debates over development and infallibility. Whether they offered explanations along logical, trans-
formationist or theological lines, those who discussed dogmatic
development took the category of dogma for granted. *Dogmengeschichte* invited their intensive examination and disagree-
ment, but they could all tell a dogma at any point in that
history where they saw one. This held true also of those who
dismiss the papal definitions of 1854 and 1950, along with Vatican I's declarations on papal infallibility and primacy, as the
issuing of false or unwarranted dogmas. These events were held

to be genuine 'dogmatic' pronouncements, albeit misguided or even sinful ones.

Hans Küng, in his questioning of any papal, ecclesiastical or biblical claims to infallibility, still takes for granted 'dogma' as an overarching category which runs from the apostolic period down to the present day. He contrasts 'self-defensive, defining statements' with 'the deliberate development of dogma, the stating of interpretative propositions'. Both the New Testament and Christian tradition justify 'defensive-defining' dogmas, when in exceptional circumstances they prove unavoidably necessary. Küng strongly disapproves of the second class of dogmas :

> It must be regarded as an aberration when a Church, without being compelled to do so, produces dogmas, whether for reasons of Church or theological policy (the two Vatican dogmas about the Pope) or for reasons of piety and propaganda (the two Vatican dogmas about Mary).

Nevertheless, he lists both classes of definitions under the general heading of 'dogma'.[1]

Even Avery Dulles, who casts proper doubt on the feasibility of trying to count the exact number of dogmas which have arisen in the history of the Church, continues to use the classification. Any list of dogmas, he suggests,

> would presumably include the declaration of Nicaea that the son is consubstantial (*homoousion*) with the Father; the definition of the First Council of Constantinople that the Holy Spirit is worthy of divine adoration; the affirmation of the Council of Chalcedon that Jesus Christ has two complete natures, divine and human; the listing of the seven sacraments by the Council of Trent; papal infallibility as defined by Vatican I; and two Marian dogmas of 1854 and 1950— the Immaculate Conception and the Assumption. This is not a complete list, or even a selection of the most important, but a mere sampling to indicate the kind of thing we are talking about when we speak of dogmas.[2]

Once again 'dogma' is allowed to serve as an umbrella term covering the full sweep of Christian history. The use of *Dogmengeschichte* in the titles of the classic studies by Harnack, Friedrich Loofs and Reinhold Seeberg on the history of doctrine carries the same implication.

Yet what else do we have here but another case of writing history backwards? It looks very much as if theologians prove here as guilty and misleading as many other academics. Thomas Kuhn remarks that 'scientists are not . . . the only group that tends to see its discipline's past developing linearly towards its present vantage. The temptation to write history backwards is both omnipresent and perennial.'[3] 'Dogma' was not a specific thing which established itself once and for all in the apostolic age and has gone on developing through the history of Christianity. Yet theologians commonly allege or imply that almost from the beginning it was essentially there. Its historical development introduced only accidental modifications.

We have become far too used to tracking down origins, pushing back further and further the line of antecedents (both good and bad), following curves of growth and decline and tracing trajectories in history. We slip easily into evolutionary and organic metaphors to assert sets of relations. We readily assume a single, great series in which, for good or ill, every dogma would take its place. Maurice Bévenot calls for the 'pruning' of dogma,[4] where others would speak of the 'de-development' or even the 'demolition' of dogma. Küng, while accepting from Newman and Johann Adam Möhler the notion of dogmatic development, criticizes some (deliberate) development of dogmas as serious aberrations, definitions produced 'just for the pleasure of defining' and not through 'pastoral necessity'.[5] But for all these writers 'dogma' remains a customary description, a self-evident reality. It allows them to fashion and retain an organized conceptual system.

What confronts us in this use of 'dogma' is yet another mis-

leading, 'retrospective re-grouping'.[6] Dogma is a recent category which can be applied to the Chalcedonian confession,
Tridentine definitions and Pius XII's proclamation of Mary's
assumption only by a retrospective hypothesis. There is a real
danger that we employ the term with about as much precision
and usefulness as new left militants speak of 'fascists'.

Let me argue this case in detail. Conciliar and papal
'definitions' did not adopt the word 'dogma' before 1870. We
noted in Chapter I how as a technical theological term it came
into use only in the course of the nineteenth century. The first
Vatican Council taught and defined papal infallibility as a
'divinely revealed dogma' (DS 3073). Pius XII used the same
expression in his 1950 definition of the assumption. In 1854,
however, Pius IX defined Mary's immaculate conception as a
revealed 'doctrine' (DS 2803). Quite consciously the bishops
at Vatican I and Pius XII set their statements under the category of 'dogma'. Yet are we only reading terminology backwards and not necessarily writing history backwards, if we apply
this category to the Councils of Trent, Chalcedon and Nicaea?
The term did not establish itself until recently. But has the kind
of thing it names been there from the earliest centuries of
Christianity? Does a regular pattern of antecedents allow us to
speak of the history of dogma?

What would count as a sufficient resemblance to link and
classify all the following items as 'dogmas': the Nicene creed, the
Chalcedonian definition, Boniface VIII's bull *Unam Sanctam*,
the Tridentine canons on justification and Pius XII's definition
of Mary's assumption? What would count as a sufficient difference to set them apart? Michel Foucault's questions may
facilitate insight into our issue:

On what 'table', according to what grid of identities, similitudes,
analogies have we become accustomed to sort out so many
different and similar things? What is this coherence—which,
as is immediately apparent, is neither determined by an

a priori and necessary concatenation, nor imposed on us by immediately perceptible contents?[7]

Before daring to pigeon-hole a great series of ecclesiastical pronouncements as 'dogmas', we need to be able to isolate, analyse, match and on good grounds finally group them all together.

It has become conventional to admit that we cannot simply juxtapose dogmas and place them in succession as if they enjoyed equal value and significance. We must remember 'the hierarchy of truths'—to recall one of those touchstone phrases which became popular after Vatican II.[8] Primary dogmas enjoy a central significance because they speak in clearer terms of the mystery of our redemption in Christ. Other (secondary) dogmas remain more peripheral. As we have seen, the 'hierarchy of truths' principle amounts to saying that all dogmas are equal, but some dogmas are more equal than others. This comes down to admitting that 'dogma' is not a univocal term. When we apply it to Chalcedon, Trent, other Councils and the pronouncements of popes, we are dealing with analogies, with statements that resemble one another but fall short of being exactly the same.

The differences between dogmas, however, are in fact so great that it looks incoherent to retain this common classification. We can readily uncover the radical discontinuities by recalling (1) the differences between speakers, (2) the variety of content and (3) the shifting mode of religious authority involved in various pronouncements which theologians commonly classify as dogmas. Let us examine first in considerable detail the differences between speakers.

Doctrines of *both* Church councils *and* popes have carried the common designation of 'dogma'. Let us leave aside disagreements about the relative theological status of councils and popes. As we have argued in the previous chapter, papal and conciliar statements fail to offer the same possibility of uncovering their *meaning*. Without many misgivings we may speak of 'the original meaning' of papal definitions. Normally we would hardly need to question a pope to be clear about his statement. The meaning he wished to convey would usually become apparent through the context, general usage and the social conventions then in force. With conciliar definitions the case is different. There the speakers offer us an ineradicable ambiguity and plurality of meaning. It is highly dubious to assume that any dogma proclaimed by any Church council ever had a single, original meaning.

Further, the *religious experience* which lies behind pronouncements from popes and councils varies hugely. Pius XII's definition of Mary's assumption, like similar papal statements, came out of the background of one Church leader's devotion. Only the mean-minded could doubt the vigour and reality of that pope's faith, even if some deem the expression of his faith to be at times misguided. Pius XII not only took final responsibility for the definition of the assumption, but he could also give an account of the personal motives, experiences and feelings which underlay his words. Where we can ascertain the motives, experiences and feelings which the bishop at Trent brought, let us say, to their endorsement of the canons on justification (DS 1551–83), we face a large and incoherent picture. Their degree of personal conviction about the beliefs they endorsed varied greatly. The formal Latin texts were hardly discriminating enough to register even a few insights, emotions and attitudes of faith which they all equally shared. The sheer fact that they gave their votes to a common document hardly constitutes sufficient evidence for concluding to a common interior state of belief. Could we argue that their dogmatic pronouncements on justification enjoyed a similar force in their thinking, because these pronouncements governed their actions in similar ways? Only a foolhardy person would risk asserting that the behaviour of the Tridentine bishops showed that they were all personally committed to the same kind of life—some fixed style of living appropriate for 'justified' Christians. In brief, their actions scarcely allow us to conclude to a uniform quality and level in their interior dispositions of belief.

Our problem about belief resembles our problem about meaning. In the last chapter we rejected the view which confidently maintains that conciliar dogmas enjoy one original meaning. Just as there is no such thing as 'the' meaning of such dogmas, so there is no such thing as 'the' faith which dogma expresses. Any simple, non-valent answer is ruled out, whenever we put two questions about dogmas deriving from Church councils. What did the fathers mean? What did they believe? Their personal paraphrases of the conciliar texts would have varied, even as their levels of spiritual awareness and personal commitment were far from uniform.

Karl Rahner calls 'a dogmatic statement' a 'statement of faith'. He understands dogmas to be addressed *ex fide ad fidem* or *ex experientia ad experientiam*.[9] In this regard popes and councils differ drastically. We can legitimately speak of a pope's faith and his religious experience, which seeks through a dogmatic pronouncement to evoke Christian faith and experience in his audience. When bishops define dogmas at a council, however, they speak *ex experientiis* and, if one may use the term, *ex fidibus*. There is no uniform or unified faith and experience out of which they address other Christians. The tag *ex fide ad fidem* glosses over a serious degree of discontinuity between papal and conciliar definitions of dogmas.

If it appears problematic to classify popes *and* councils together as authors of dogmas, difficulties also arise when we seek to group (1) councils *with* councils, or (2) popes *with* popes. The diversity comes through once we ask : Who was it that spoke and to whom? Three examples of papal 'dogmas' show how both speaker and audience vary : Leo I's *Tome to Flavian* on the relationship of the divinity and humanity in Christ, Boniface VIII's bull *Unam Sanctam* on the necessity of subjection to the pope and Pius XII's apostolic constitution *Munificentissimus Deus* on Mary's assumption. Leo I wrote his letter to Flavian the bishop of Constantinople. At the Council of Chalcedon which the Emperor Marcian convoked in 451 the letter was read and acclaimed by the bishops : 'Peter has spoken through Leo. This is the teaching of Cyril. Anathema to him that believes otherwise.' (The

'Cyril' was, of course, the recently deceased Cyril of Alexandria. For the bishops it was primarily 'Peter', not Christ, who spoke through the pope.) Leo's *Tome* appeared during the final period of the Roman Empire. Besides going to Flavian and the fathers at Chalcedon, it went also to the Council of Ephesus in 449 (which Leo later castigated as the 'Robber Council') and to a synod held at Milan in 451. The Arian king of the Vandals, Geiseric, four years later pillaged Rome. The *Tome* was not addressed to him in the hopes of correcting his heterodoxy or curbing his devastation of the Empire. Nor was it addressed to Christians in faraway places like St Patrick, who was apparently then evangelizing parts of Ireland. Leo intended his *Tome* to correct the extreme 'Alexandrianism' of an elderly monk of Constantinople, Eutyches, who took Cyril of Alexandria's doctrine to entail only one nature in Christ.

Through his bull *Unam Sanctam* the medieval pope Boniface VIII spoke to a situation which gravely threatened his spiritual authority. Philip IV of France, who had already cut off the flow of French revenues to Rome, reacted by seizing and briefly imprisoning the pope who died a few weeks later. Although the bull was addressed to the universal Church, it was not everywhere disseminated at the time. If it reached Ireland, it would not have been automatically welcome. Another bull, Pope Adrian IV's *Laudabiliter*, had earlier declared it praiseworthy that the English king Henry II should enter and establish order in Ireland, provided he secured the rights of the Church and contributed tribute to Rome. Henry proceeded to visit Ireland in 1171-2 to secure his power there.

Pius XII addressed his definition of Mary's assumption to 'the Church universal'. Through radio, newspapers, the co-operation of bishops and the work of other groups, news of the definition spread quickly to its intended world-wide audience. In Ireland, for instance, the bishops directed that on November 19, 1950, the text of the dogma was to be 'read and explained at all Masses in all churches and chapels, so that congregations could profess their acceptance of it'.[10] This modern pope enjoyed an instant and far-flung audience that had been denied to his predecessors in medieval and Roman times.

We ride roughshod over many historical differences between these bishops of Rome, if we classify Leo I, Boniface VIII and Pius XII together as having each once produced a 'dogma'. This obliges us to see properly fulfilled in their pronouncements the following requirements : (1) They were concerned with a divinely revealed truth, (2) which they proclaimed as such on the basis of their infallible teaching authority, (3) intending their proclamation to bind all the faithful forever. We manage to juxtapose the *Tome to Flavian*, *Unam Sanctam* and *Munificentissimus Deus* and allot them the same logical status, only if we are ready to deal with legal abstractions and play down in each case the historical conditions of speaker and audience. Did Leo have any intention of 'binding' *all* the faithful both then and forever by his fraternal letter to Flavian? Was Boniface dealing with divinely revealed truth, when he declared that 'subjection to the Roman Pontiff is absolutely necessary for salvation—for every human being'?

In comparing the three 'dogmas', we may not overlook the diverse ways in which Leo, Boniface and Pius came to speak with the authority of bishop of Rome. When Leo was away on a mission to Gaul, Pope Sixtus III died in 440 and the people of Rome elected Leo. On his return to the city he was consecrated bishop. Boniface, who had become a cardinal priest in 1291, three years later helped to persuade Pope Celestine V to resign and went on to be elected pope at the conclave of cardinals that followed. Pius XII, already the cardinal secretary of state, succeeded almost automatically when Pius XI died in 1939. Leo I, Boniface VIII and Pius XII travelled different routes to be empowered to speak with papal authority. Pius was born pope, Boniface achieved papacy and Leo had papacy thrust upon him.

The differences between the status of speakers seem enormous when we compare councils of the Church. The bishops at Chalcedon represented and addressed an undivided Christendom. Vatican I failed to represent the Orthodox, Protestant and Anglican Churches. If Trent has proved to be the most significant western ecumenical council, only a few dozen 'fathers' participated in important sessions. More than six hundred bishops attended the Council of Chalcedon, while Vatican I drew around eight hundred. The Roman Emperors convoked the first seven councils which both the Catholic and Orthodox Churches regard as ecumenical. Constantine I presided over the sessions at the Council of Nicaea and prescribed the subjects for discussion. Pope Pius IX, however, convoked Vatican I, determined the order of business and gave the final approval for the promulgation of the conciliar decrees. The first seven councils admitted princes, their ambassadors, abbots, and representatives of religious institutes, as well as bishops. At Vatican I both attendance and the right to vote were restricted to cardinals, bishops and the heads of religious orders. It seems that women have never voted at councils. Half its members have been regularly excluded from what were supposedly general councils of the universal Church. Even if we consider only the methods of convoking councils, the representative nature of eligible participants and the actual numbers present, 'ecumenical' councils come across as events of different kinds. They vary hugely in their claim to speak *for* the Church or be heard *by* one Church. The conclusion imposes itself. It is questionable to group together the speakers of Nicaea, Chalcedon, Trent and Vatican I as delivering the same authoritative product —'dogmas'.

We have dwelt at length on the differences between those who have uttered what have been classified under the common heading of 'dogmas'. We can uncover further radical discontinuities by noting the variety of content and the shifting modes of religious authority involved in papal and conciliar pronouncements usually lumped together as 'dogmas'. In Chapter III we observed how the descriptive and prescriptive functions of dogmatic pronouncements remain anything but constant. The doxological character can likewise vary greatly. At the risk of putting matters in a simple-minded way, we might say that Chalcedon praised Christ, Vatican I acclaimed papal authority and Pius XII in *Munificentissimus Deus* glorified the Virgin Mary. One hardly needs to be particularly sensitive to historical nuances to see how both the style and the status of authoritative conciliar and papal teaching have shifted. Through its intrinsic worth Leo I's *Tome to Flavian* spread widely and won assured authority, even though in itself it was no more than a letter from 'Bishop Leo' to his 'beloved brother Flavian, Bishop of Constantinople (*Leo episcopus dilectissimo fratri flaviano Constantinopolitano episcopo*)'. Boniface VIII's *Unam Sanctam* became at once and has remained an embarrassment, a titanic claim to papal control over human salvation. 'By the authority of Our Lord Jesus Christ, and of his blessed Apostles Peter and Paul, and by the authority granted to us', Pius XII proclaimed the 'dogma' of Mary's assumption (DS 3903), and won instant acclaim from the Roman Catholic world. By forcing together Leo's *Tome*, *Unam Sanctam* and *Munificentissimus Deus* under the common heading of 'dogma', we are bringing together strange bedfellows. The anathematizing of opposing errors which has regularly followed solemn formulations of faith varied greatly. Trent hurled anathemas at such identifiable opponents as John Calvin and Martin Luther. The anathemas that followed Pius IX's proclamation of the immaculate conception and, even more clearly, those which Pius XII included in *Munificentissimus Deus* formally continued a tradition, but were not aimed at concrete persons. So-called 'dogmas' have varied immensely not only in their positive teaching, but also in the tone and methods with which they excluded errors.

If we continue to use dogma in its technical theological sense, it is an uncertain unity, an unserviceable category for drawing together such pronouncements as the Chalcedonian definition, *Unam Sanctam* and the Tridentine canons. If we decide to use it in a looser and more popular sense, we deal with a pejorative term. It is interesting to note how Ronald Knox's sensitivity over this issue led him to translate as 'doctrine' the Latin word *dogma* in *Munificentissimus Deus*.[11] Theologians hardly want to speak of 'dogma' in its popular sense. Even in its technical meaning they ought to relegate the word to the museum. This category requires, not purification, but elimination.

Let me state clearly what I am *not* arguing. I am not rejecting the *translation* of terminology. Obviously our classifications were often unavailable to previous generations. What they said and the procedures they went through in saying what they said can sometimes be legitimately translated into modern terms. Is this so in the case of the recent concept of 'dogma'? Did the Council of Nicaea, Leo I, Boniface VIII, the Council of Trent and Pius XII *all* mean to do what we would call 'defining a dogma'? That is the question I am answering with an emphatic 'No!'. It is a delusion to imagine that there are sufficient common elements in all the conciliar and papal pronouncements we recall to group them under our one term, 'dogma'. There are some similarities and relationships, but nothing satisfactorily common to all. 'Dogma' has been woven into the fabric of modern theology. Sanctioned by time and repetition, it seduces us into thinking that as a specific thing it has gone on developing since early Christianity, and that the development eventually led up to the formal identification of this category. We are guilty of writing history backwards through an anachronistic classification.

The title of this book asked: Has dogma a future? In this concluding chapter I answer: It did not have a past. There were no 'dogmas'. This persistent and prominent word misrepresents the past when it serves as an umbrella term covering the full sweep of Christian history. What can we put in its place? We can, in the first place, respect and reproduce the nomenclature used by the councils and popes in question. They describe their authoritative statements as canons, decrees, bulls, confessions, symbols, doctrines and—very recently—dogmas. Obviously we need to be cautious. Translation and usage have altered the meaning of these terms. The denotations and connotations of 'canons' differ from the Tridentine use of *canones*. Nevertheless, we may recall the terminology Trent used to describe its solemn decisions, provided we refrain from reading our meaning(s) into it. Second, a general term with very little propositional content could serve to bring together various papal and conciliar pronouncements. We might speak of teachings or formulations of faith. These terms could be applied to the texts from Nicaea, Chalcedon, Trent, Pius IX and Pius XII, without lapsing into a misleading form of retrospective re-grouping. It seems better to avoid 'doctrine(s)'. The pejorative implications of being 'doctrinaire' lie too close at hand.

Does the rejection of the category of 'dogma' entail an unexpected abandonment of the case for 'dogma' argued earlier in this book—specifically, in Chapters III and IV? There we maintained that our inherited 'dogmas' could act as guides and incentives to genuinely Christian living. Those arguments can be applied without much trouble to Church canons, papal bulls, conciliar confessions and all the other items from the past normally lumped together as 'dogmas'. Conciliar confessions, for instance, can describe the relationship of Christ to his Father and prescribe our response in faith to that mysterious truth. There is no need to apply the anachronistic category of 'dogma' to such confessions, before my account of the functions and limitations of such language can work.

It was somewhat evasive to answer the question posed by the title of this book by saying : 'Dogma did not have a past.' What of the future? Dogma *may* have a future, but only if coming Church councils and popes decide to fulfil in a uniform fashion the exact procedures required by the modern concept of dogma. Pius XII did just that in defining Mary's assumption. Vatican II declined to follow his lead. Although a future growth of dogmas cannot be absolutely ruled out, nevertheless, short formulations of faith, creeds and other means of proclaiming and confessing the Christian message look preferable. Could dogmas ever again prove really necessary to defend the true faith and decide on Church membership? First, no one can argue that only dogmas can properly safeguard faith. St Paul took his gospel seriously and at times uttered a loud 'No !', but did not introduce dogmatic formulations. I Peter suggests quiet witness to the truth : 'Should anyone ask you the reason for this hope of yours, be ever ready to reply, but speak gently and respectfully' (3 : 15f.). Defence through dialogue has, in fact, largely replaced defence through anathema.

Second, who would welcome a return to the situation where Church leaders impose dogmatic formulations to separate heretics from the orthodox? Christian faith must be a Church faith. But methods for preserving the faith of the Church must also be Christian. Was it ever Christian to impose verbal acceptance of formulas under pain of exclusion from Church office or even Church membership? In a Church which first became genuinely world-wide since the sixteenth century, common formulations look less and less plausible. The diversity of languages, cultures and thought-forms rule out such formulations—at least for those Christians who refuse to cling to the past and endorse that classic piece of chauvinism : 'Europe is the faith and the faith is Europe.' Common dogmas are far from being the sole method of reaching mutual understanding between believers. Those who agree that believing *in* Christ takes precedence over believing *that* certain truths are the case will look for orthopraxy in their fellow-Christians. Vatican I pointed in that direction by its claims about the holiness and good practice of the Catholic Church (DS 3013). Orthopraxy serves as a criterion for orthodoxy. Rather than simply noting that someone uses the 'right' words, we should observe what these words lead him to do or leave undone. 'None of those who cry out, "Lord, Lord", will enter the kingdom of God but only the one who does the will of my Father in heaven' (Matt 7 : 21). 'Christopraxy' serves to identify genuinely orthodox Christology. Not everyone who recites the Chalcedonian confession really believes in Christ. Verbally correct Christology can cloak a highly deficient Christopraxy.[12]

For the future one can only hope that the Church as a whole will agree to dispense with dogma. Whether that will happen or not, at least the past history of Christianity has not left us with a major task of de-dogmatization. Dehellenization in the sense of a strict de-dogmatization of Christianity is delusory talk. We have been seduced by Harnack and other theologians into thinking that from the earliest centuries there developed a great series of solemn Church statements, which in the modern technical sense must be called 'dogmas'.

Theologians are not spokesmen for God. It is simply that they watch their language in the presence of God. One can put this point less solemnly. Theologians, no less than philosophers, are bound by Wittgenstein's charge to 'battle against the bewitchment of our intelligence by means of language'. In this book, I aimed to watch my dogmatic language in the presence of God *and* man. Ultimately I can only conclude that 'dogma' must be dropped, because it is a bewitchment of our intelligence rather than an outrage against our Christian lives.

Notes

—————

Abbreviations: DS *Enchiridion Symbolorum, definitionum et declarationum de rebus fidei et morum*, ed. H. Denzinger, rev. A. Schönmetzer, 32nd ed. (Freiburg).

ET English translation.

Introduction

1 M. E. Williams, 'Dogma', *New Catholic Encyclopedia*, 4, p. 948.
2 For a useful bibliography see N. Lash, *Change in Focus* (London, 1973), pp. 183–91.
3 ET : London, 1971.
4 For a useful bibliography and summary see A. Houtepen, 'A Hundred Years after Vatican I : Some Light on the Concept of Infallibility', *Concilium* vol. 3, no. 9 (March, 1973), pp. 124–8.
5 See the fresh debate on this problem occasioned by L. Dewart's *The Future of Belief* (London, 1967).

Chapter I

1 See A. Dulles, *The Survival of Dogma* (New York, 1971), p. 153.
2 *Principles of Christian Theology* (London, 1966), pp. 164–5.
3 *Unfolding Revelation* (London, 1972), p. 38; italics mine.
4 *The Christian Tradition*, I, *The Emergence of the Catholic Tradition* (Chicago, 1971), p. 4.
5 *Leitfaden zum Studium der Dogmengeschichte*, ed. K. Aland (6 ed. : Tübingen, 1959), I, p. 9.
6 *Lehrbuch der Dogmengeschichte* (5 ed. : Tübingen, 1931), I, p. 3.

7 On these two approaches to revelation see my *Foundations of Theology* (Chicago, 1971), pp. 23ff.

Chapter II

1 *The Vanity of Dogmatizing* (London, 1961), pp. 229f.
2 *The Survival of Dogma*, pp. 176, 181.
3 B. Russell, *Why I am not a Christian* (London, 1957), p. xiii.
4 *Ibid.*, p. 180.
5 *Ibid.*, p. 169f.
6 *The Australian* for May 25, 1970.
7 (ET : London, 1933), pp. 143f.
8 *Letters and Papers from Prison* (ET : London, 1971), pp. 280, 286.
9 *Commonitorium* 2, PL 50 : 640.
10 'On the Historical Structure of Christian Truth', *Heythrop Journal* 9 (1968), p. 134.
11 *The Vanity of Dogmatizing*, pp. 230f.
12 II-II, q. 1, a. 2, ad 2; see E. Schillebeeckx, 'The Problem of the Infallibility of the Church's Office', *Concilium* vol. 3, no. 9 (March 1973), pp. 90f.
13 Boston, 1971.
14 *Lehrbuch der Dogmengeschichte*, I, pp. 20, 698.
15 *Essays Philosophical and Theological* (ET : London, 1955), pp. 280, 286.
16 *The Future of Belief*, pp. 77–121.
17 *Ibid.*, p. 133.
18 *Jesus in Bad Company* (ET : London, 1972), pp. 42f.
19 *Medievalism* (London, 1908), p. 10.
20 Art. 14ff.; cf. DS 3866–73.
21 *Contribution to the Critique of Hegel's Philosophy of Right* (ET : New York, 1964), p. 44.
22 August 26, 1950.
23 *The System of Nature*, I (ET : London, 1797), pp. xi–xii.

Chapter III

1 W. H. Austin, 'Religious Commitment and the Logical Status of Doctrine', *Religious Studies* 9 (1973), p. 39.
2 DS 301–02.
3 A. Flew and A. MacIntyre (eds), *New Essays in Philosophical Theology* (London, 1969), p. 98.

4 *Truth*, ed. G. Pitcher (Englewood Cliffs, N.J., 1964), p. 45.
5 *Theological Investigations*, 5 (ET : London, 1966), pp. 45f.
6 *New Catholic Encyclopedia*, 4, p. 948.
7 *Historical Theology* (London, 1971), p. 20.
8 *Theological Investigations*, 5, p. 51.

Chapter IV

1 Since the Council of Trent some theologians have maintained that Church tradition could 'contain' some revealed truths not found in the scriptures. Hence dogmatic definitions of these truths would add something to the scriptural record. In this regard dogma could enjoy a priority over scripture. This post-Tridentine view, however, has lost ground; it understands both revelation and tradition in a defective fashion. See J. Ratzinger and K. Rahner, *Revelation and Tradition* (ET : Freiburg, 1966) and my own *Theology and Revelation* (Cork, 1968), pp. 74ff.
2 *Historical Theology*, p. 95.
3 *Adventures of Ideas* (Cambridge, 1933), p. 66.
4 Nicolas Lash puts this principle more elegantly : 'There are moments in the history of christian tradition when the church confesses its faith with peculiar precisiveness, confidence and clarity, and . . . the affirmations thus made remain—in different ways, and in varying degrees—normative for subsequent belief and exploration' (*Change in Focus*, p. 181).
5 *Theological Investigations*, 1 (ET : London, 1961), p. 149.
6 *Method in Theology* (London, 1972), p. 4; italics mine.
7 *Theological Investigations*, 5, p. 25.
8 *The Vanity of Dogmatizing*, p. 230.
9 *The Misery of Christianity* (ET : London, 1971), p. 143.
10 *Lehrbuch der Dogmengeschichte*, I, p. 20.
11 'The Dehellenization of Dogma', *Theological Studies* 28 (1967), pp. 345ff.
12 *Psychology and Religion* (ET : London, 1970), p. 50.
13 *On Heresy* (ET : Freiburg, 1964), p. 54.
14 On the need for reformulation see Avery Dulles' excellent treatment in *The Survival of Dogma*, pp. 185–203.
15 See P. Fransen, *Die Interpretation des Dogmas*, ed. P. Schoonenberg (Düsseldorf, 1969), pp. 114ff.
16 *But that I can't believe* (London, 1967), pp. 86f.
17 *Method in Theology*, p. 305.
18 *The Theology of Secularity* (Dublin, 1974), pp. 79ff.

Chapter V

1 'On the Historical Structure of Christian Truth', *Heythrop Journal* 9 (1968), pp. 279–80. Vass realizes that it runs 'contrary to the accepted usage of logic' to call 'certain interpretative questions "true or untrue"' (*ibid.*, p. 279).

2 *Change in Focus*, p. 178; italics mine.

3 Address by Pius XII on November 1, 1950; from *The Tablet* for November 4, 1950.

4 M. F. Wiles argues that the clue to interpreting doctrinal development lies in 'a continuity of fundamental aims' and not, therefore, necessarily in any continuity of meaning. There could be and in fact has been a good deal of both change and sheer error in doctrinal affirmations (*The Making of Christian Doctrine* [Cambridge, 1967], pp. 172f.). In this account objectives matter more than meaning, which could be true or false. Might we say that for Professor Wiles the end justifies, or at least excuses, the (frequently erroneous) meaning?

5 Letter to *The Times* for September 14, 1950. The statement which the Irish hierarchy directed to be read at all public Masses on October 29, 1950, exemplified the belief to which Selwyn objected : 'The definition [sc. of the assumption] . . . will bring all Christians to pray more fervently for Mary's help, that, as formerly she saved Europe at Lepanto and Vienna, so now, in a peril more terrible, she may comfort and protect Christians in every land against the attacks of God's enemies' (from *The Tablet* for October 21, 1950).

6 *Meaning and Truth* (Oxford, 1970), p. 5.

7 *Change in Focus*, pp. 174f.; italics mine.

8 *Method in Theology*, pp. 325f.

9 From *The Tablet* for November 4, 1950.

10 November 6, 1950.

11 *Psychology and Religion*, p. 467.

12 *Ibid.*, pp. 463, 465.

13 *Ibid.*, p. 462.

14 *Theological Investigations*, 1, p. 215. The German original speaks of 'content (Inhalt)' of the dogma, but Rahner's discussion of content amounts to a shift of meaning.

15 'Symptoms and Causes of the Present Crisis in Religious Language', *Concilium* vol. 5, no. 9 (May 1973), p. 12.

16 *The Archaeology of Knowledge* (ET : London, 1972), pp. 109–10.

Chapter VI

1 *Infallible? An Enquiry*, pp. 120–2.
2 *The Survival of Dogma*, p. 153.
3 *The Structure of Scientific Revolutions* (Chicago, 1962), p. 137.
4 'Primacy and Development', *Heythrop Journal* 9 (1968), pp. 407f.
5 *Infallible? An Enquiry*, pp. 122f.
6 M. Foucault, *The Archaeology of Knowledge*, p. 31.
7 *The Order of Things* (ET : London, 1970), p. xix.
8 'In Catholic teaching there exists an order or "hierarchy" of truths, since they vary in their relationship to the foundation of the Christian faith' (Vatican II, *Decree on Ecumenism*, art. 11). U. Valeske traces the history of this theological commonplace in his *Hierarchia Veritatum* (Munich, 1968).
9 *Theological Investigations*, 5, p. 48.
10 *The Tablet*, October 29, 1950.
11 *Ibid.*, December 23, 1950.
12 I owe the distinction between Christology and Christopraxy to Josef Nolte, *Grund und Grenzen des Dogmas* (Freiburg, 1973), pp. 94ff.

Very Select Bibliography

A. Deneffe, 'Dogma : Worte und Begriff', *Scholastik* 6 (1931), pp. 381–400.

A. Dulles, *The Survival of Dogma* (New York, 1971).

G. Ebeling, 'The Word of God and Church Doctrine', *The Word of God and Tradition* (ET : London, 1968), pp. 160–80.

M. Elze, 'Der Begriff des Dogmas in der alten Kirche', *Zeitschrift für Theologie und Kirche* 61 (1964), pp. 421–38.

W. Joest and W. Pannenberg (eds.), *Dogma und Denkstrukturen* (Göttingen, 1963).

W. Kasper, *Dogma unter dem Wort Gottes* (Mainz, 1965).

J. Nolte, *Dogma in Geschichte* (Freiburg, 1971).

——, 'Tradition and Praxis. Zur Frage nach dem Ort des Dogmas innerhalb einer Theologisichen Kriteriologie', *Grund und Grenzen des Dogmas* by H. Feld et al. (Freiburg, 1973), pp. 77–99.

W. Pannenberg, 'What is a Dogmatic Statement', *Basic Questions in Theology*, I (ET : London, 1970), pp. 182–210.

K. Rahner, 'Considerations on the Development of Dogma', *Theological Investigations*, IV (ET : London, 1966), pp. 3–35.

——, 'The Development of Dogma', *ibid.*, I (ET : London, 1961), pp. 39–77.

——, 'What is a Dogmatic Statement?', *ibid.*, V (ET : London, 1966), pp. 42–66.

E. Schlink, 'The Structure of Dogmatic Statements as an Ecumenical Problem', *The Coming Christ and the Coming Church* (ET : Edinburgh, 1967), pp. 16–84.

P. Schoonenberg (ed.), *Die Interpretation des Dogmas* (Düsseldorf, 1969).

M. F. Wiles, *The Making of Christian Doctrine* (Cambridge, 1967).

——, *The Remaking of Christian Doctrine* (London, 1974).

Index of Names

Aquinas, St. Thomas, 16, 20, 37, 48 f.
Augustine, St., 1, 48, 58

Barth, K., 14
Bévenot, M., 88
Bonhoeffer, D., 14
Boniface VIII, Pope, 6, 19, 70 f., 76 f., 81, 89, 92 ff.
Bultmann, R., 17

Calvin, J., 10, 96
Cyril of Alexandria, St., 92 f.

Dewart, L., 17, 101
Dulles, A., xii, 10, 87, 101, 103, 107

Eliot, T. S., 47, 49

Flew, A., 24 f., 102
Foucault, M., 83, 89, 105
Freud, S., 43, 60

Glanvill, J., 9 f., 15, 52

Harnack, A., xiii, 4, 17 f., 59, 88, 100

Holbach, P. Thiry d', 21 f., 67
Holl, A., 17 f.

Jesus Christ, *passim*
Jung, C. G., 61, 68, 80 ff.

Kahl, J., 58 f.
Kierkegaard, S., 43, 60
Knox, R. A., 96 f.
Kuhn, T., 88
Küng, H., xii, 87 f.

Lash, N., xiii, 71, 76 f., 81, 101, 103
Leo I, Pope St., 1, 92 ff., 96 f.
Lonergan, B., 48, 59, 64, 79
Loofs, F., 4, 88
Luther, M., 48, 96

Macquarrie, J., 3, 23
Martindale, C. C., 80 f.
Marx, K., 20, 67
Mauriac, F., 80 f.

Newman, J. H., xii, 88
Nolte, J., xiii, 105, 107

Pascal, B., 48, 60

Paul, St., 1, 12, 16, 41, 50, 54 ff.
  60, 70, 99
Pelikan, J., xii, 4, 35
Pius IX, Pope, 2 f., 6, 53, 84,
  95 ff.
Pius XII, Pope, xi, 21, 36,
  70–84 *passim*, 89, 91 f., 94,
  96 ff., 104
Priscillian, 9 f.

Rahner, K., xii, 23, 30, 38,
  47, 62, 81 f., 92, 103, 105,
  107
Robinson, J. A. T., 64

Russell, B., 13, 15, 102

Schlink, E., xii, 39, 107
Schönmetzer, A., 69, 101
Selwyn, E. G., 74
Strawson, P. F., 25 f., 75

Vass, G., 14, 70, 104
Virgin Mary, the, *passim*

Whitehead, A. N., 44 f.
Wiles, M. F., xiii, 104, 107
Williams, M. E., 33, 101